CHEDDAR VALLEY RAILWAY WALK

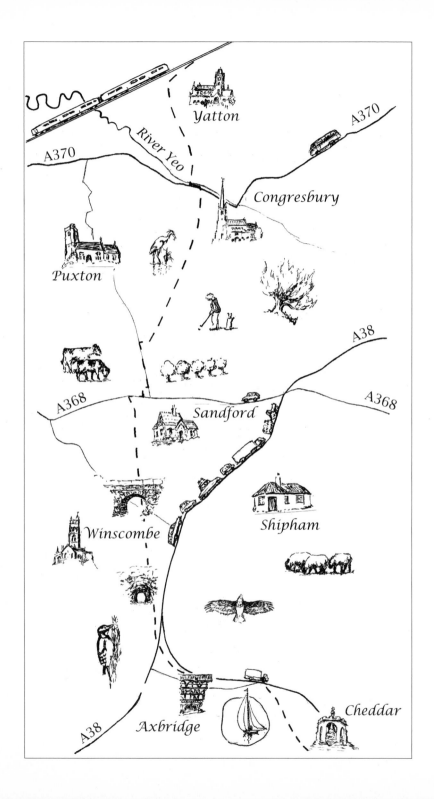

CHEDDAR VALLEY RAILWAY WALK

*History and Walks along the former
Cheddar Valley Railway Line*

Douglas Kidder &
Amanda Brading

EX LIBRIS PRESS

Published in 1999 by EX LIBRIS PRESS
1 The Shambles   Bradford on Avon
Wiltshire   BA15 1JS

Design and typesetting by
Ex Libris Press

Typeset in 10/13.5 Lucida Bright

Cover printed by
Shires Press, Trowbridge, Wiltshire

Printed in Britain by
Cromwell Press, Trowbridge, Wiltshire

ISBN 0 948578 44 0

Acknowledgements
We are grateful to Pauline Wathen for permission to use railway
photographs taken by her late husband Malcolm, and to Ursula
Richmond for the use of photographs of the line after closure taken
by her late husband Donald. We would also like to thank Peter Knight
for information about the Cheddar Valley Railway, and William
Stanton for advice on the geology of the Mendips.

The range of walks would have been smaller without the efforts
of the very many members and friends who helped to provide or
check the routes. Thanks are also due to many others who helped us
in a vanety of ways.

Credits
The photographs of the working railways are by Malcolm Wathen
and those of the derelict railway by Donald Richmond. The maps,
line drawings and poems are by Douglas Kidder. The steel engravings
are from an old edition of Chambers Encyclopaedia.

CONTENTS

Above: The coach on the left is on the Clevedon Line. The train centre is on the main line ready to go on to Weston-super-Mare. The train on the right is in the bay of the Cheddar Valley Line which is seen going off to the right.

Below: The line in use south of the tunnel (photo courtesy of Bunty Tracy).

1 THE CHEDDAR VALLEY RAILWAY

Creating the Line

During the second half of last century a number of competing companies were building railways throughout the country, most of which radiated from London. In Somerset the companies then planned to transport passengers and goods between the Dorset coast and the industrial areas of South Wales, the Midlands and the North by building north-south routes to cross the east-west main lines already built, so completing the web.

On July 4th, 1864, the Somerset and Dorset Railway Company obtained authorisation by Act of Parliament for the construction of a railway from Yatton to Wells, a route which also interested the Bristol and Exeter Railway Company. Both companies were by then coming across a familiar obstacle - money, or rather the lack of it. Commercial pressures had already forced some smaller companies to close or merge, and even some of the larger ones were beginning to co-operate rather than compete everywhere. So, after attempting to open routes from the Bristol Channel to the Dorset Coast in competition with one another, the Bristol & Exeter and the Somerset & Dorset Railway Companies ultimately agreed to a deal giving the B & E the right to a construct a line from Yatton to Wells, while the S & D would continue the route to the south coast.

Francis Fox, Chief Engineer to the B & E, and his brother, John H. Fox, planned and supervised the B & E portion which was initially called 'The Yatton and Cheddar Valley Line'. The Fox brothers, both old Scholars of Sidcot School, a Quaker foundation close to the chosen route, decided to tackle the tunnel first, this being the most difficult (and the most expensive) task along the route, which would otherwise hold up completion. Mrs Yatman carried out the cutting of the 'First Sod' on February 26th, 1867 at the spot chosen for the tunnel entrance, which was near Winscombe Hall, the residence of Colonel and Mrs Yatman. This ceremony, in the presence of the Mayor and Corporation of Axbridge, was followed by a procession and celebration, the liveliness of which dismayed the Quaker engineers in charge.

The Fox brothers cannily allowed for the likelihood of a change from the broad gauge used when the line was laid, to what Brunel called narrow gauge, but which everybody else by then called standard gauge. They laid cross sleepers instead of the longitudinal sleepers which were normally used on broad gauge lines so that, due to their foresight, when the route was converted to standard gauge a few years after opening, the changeover was completed in four days.

Teams of 'navvies' did the work – the term being an abbreviation for 'navigators', teams like this having been assembled in the canal building era half a century earlier. The navvies came from country areas where employment prospects were poor, which at that time meant especially Ireland and Scotland. They had an alarming, but not altogether justified reputation for drunkenness. The relative absence of problems in the villages along the line was credited at the time to the influence of the Chaplain, the Reverend W. Barclay.

The teams laid the track progressively from Yatton southwards. From there until a little short of Sandford the terrain is level and low-lying, intersected by drainage ditches called 'rhynes'.They laid hardcore to sufficient depth to raise the track above the level of the surrounding, dug drainage ditches along both sides of the track and connected these to the local rhynes, building substantial culverts at intervals to let water flow from one side to the other. Ditches along both sides of the track were a feature of most of the line, but the repeated culverts were only required in this Yatton-Sandford stretch.

The only major engineering works needed in this section were at Congresbury. Here they built a bridge to take the railway over the river Yeo, followed immediately by another to take the main Bristol to Weston-super-Mare road over the railway which then entered the site of Congresbury Station, initially built with just one platform.

At Sandford the track-layers reached the Mendip Hills, and for the next few miles had to construct alternate cuttings and embankments and at Winscombe Hill, as we have seen, a tunnel. They took the line over three main roads with bridges made of Mendip stone, and took minor roads and lanes over the track with similar smaller bridges, and put accomodation bridges or cattle creeps under the embankments where farms had been divided by the line. The first of these main roads was on the route from Weston-super-Mare to Bath, which they bridged just outside Sandford, building the station, which they called Sandford & Banwell, immediately south of the bridge.

The next main road the Fox Brothers' team had to bridge was the one from Weston-super-Mare to Wells, which they crossed in the hamlet of Woodborough, again building a station close to the bridge, this time on the north side. They originally called this Woodborough Station but owing to confusion with Woodborough in Wiltshire, rapidly renamed it Winscombe Station after the slightly larger village on a nearby hill.

The line was then routed just to the east of the old Winscombe village with its impressive church tower, to enter the north side of Winscombe Hill, which lay in front of the lowest and shortest gap in the hills, with Shute Shelve on one side and Wavering Down on the other. Navvies dug the 180 yard long tunnel, mainly with picks and shovels, but assisted in the rock section with drills and 'black powder', the traditional gunpowder explosive. The northern and central parts were through Keuper marl but the southern end had to be cut through hard Carboniferous Limestone interspersed with layers of shale. While the walls and roof in the limestone end were self-supporting, the part through the marl had to be lined. They used stone blocks, mainly in the walls, and bricks, mainly in the roof, and making the lined part narrower with recesses at intervals to produce 'refuges' for railway employees who might, in due course, be working in the tunnel when trains were passing.

The rock taken out in digging the tunnel was handy for the embankments needed for much of the remaining distance to Cheddar. Across this part of the route lay the most important of the main roads, the highway from London to Exeter via Bristol. This they bridged between Sidcot and Cross, where the line left Wavering Down and moved on to the side of Shute Shelve. A mile further on came Axbridge Station, built on the hillside a flight of steps above the ancient Saxon town. Past Axbridge the line went downhill to Cheddar, passing the site of the palace of the Kings of Wessex.

The line was opened to Cheddar on August 3rd, 1869 and the continuation to Wells on April 5th, 1870. In November, 1875 the line was converted to the narrower standard gauge and on June 1st, 1876, along with the rest of the Bristol and Exeter Railway Company, became part of the Great Western Railway

The Line in Use

Commercially the line started so successfully that the Company rapidly replaced temporary fittings by something more permanent. Where the stations had initially been constructed in wood, these were replaced by buildings of the same Mendip stone that they had used for the bridges and the tunnel. The stations, while differing in size and complexity, then all had similar stonework and the same Bristol & Exeter chalet style roofs with orange tiles and handsome bargeboards. The bridges had an even greater similarity to one another, being built to the same basic design, differing in little other than size. The overall effect was to give an identity to the line.

To permit further extension of the railway network into

Above: Cheddar Station, last regular train 7 September 1963.
Below: Steaming into Yatton.

the countryside, Parliament passed the Light Railways Act in 1896, allowing railways to be built to less stringent specifications in rural areas. In 1898 the Great Western Railway took advantage of this to build the Wrington Vale Light Railway, which left the Cheddar Valley Line at Congresbury, which became the only junction on the line. The light railway had stations at Wrington and Burrington with a halt between at Havyat Green on the A38, and continued to Blagdon where a reservoir was about to be constructed. This line was opened on November 23rd, 1901.

Near the station at Woodborough which had been renamed 'Winscombe' and rebuilt in stone in 1904, traders opened shops, a garage and a Station Hotel. Houses were then built near the shops, till the hamlet of Woodborough became a village absorbing old Winscombe in the south and Sidcot in the east. The newly created village was soon called Winscombe, after the station.

In July 1915, Sir John Jackson Ltd, the owners of Sandford Quarry, built a private rail and siding which joined the line just south of Sandford Station, so that they could load their stone into trucks in the quarry to go anywhere in the country without reloading. A similar arrangement (still working in 1998) at Merehead on the East Somerset Railway beyond Wells, allowed stone from the quarry there to go on to the national railway network. Apart from stone, the main heavy cargo was coal, considerable quantities being brought in to supply the whole area.

Dairy farmers in the area sent a great deal of their milk on the line, mostly to London, but also to Bristol and to a milk-processing factory at Yatton. Mr R.H. Mabbett of Nut Tree Farm, Winscombe, who regularly took 17 gallon churns to the station, remembered collecting a bull bought from Guernsey at Winscombe Station although the usual cattle loading bay was at Sandford.

Other farm produce included anemones going to the North in the Winter, but particularly, strawberries going in all directions in the Summer. Strawberry growers in Cheddar and neighbouring parishes on the southern slopes of Mendip used the railway to such an extent that it became known as the 'Strawberry Line'. Most of these were loaded at Cheddar, but the other stations along the line were used. Mary Killen, who was then at Townsend Farm, Axbridge, remembers picking strawberries at 5 a.m. and taking them to Axbridge station to catch the first train, with similar arrangements being made in Winter for anemones. In either case they would reach the Midlands, the North, or even Scotland the same day, to be sold in the market next morning. For a few weeks in Summer the trains often ran late because of the time taken to load the strawberries. The wide assortment of other goods carried included cattle food coming in and potatoes going out.

Large numbers of passengers travelled both locally, and to and from the main line, including commuters going to work and visitors joining the seasonal holiday trade. Very many people have memories of a route which they regarded variously as gloriously picturesque, excruciatingly slow or simply very useful.

Pupils from two schools regularly travelled on the line. The Fox brothers who engineered the line were old scholars of Sidcot School near Winscombe, and for many years this school hired a special train at the beginning and end of term. Olive Litten, of Shipham, a scholar in the 1920's, remembers that they walked from Winscombe Station to the school while the trunks went up in a cart pulled by a horse called Tom. Pupils from nearby villages travelled daily in what they called the 'Cheddar Slug'. They could see and hear these trains from the school grounds, puffing their way between Winscombe Station and the tunnel. At the crossroads overlooked by the school was the 'Sidcot Stores', now a private house, but then a flourishing business selling, among other things, sweets. When Barbara Chainey, running this family store, heard the hoot of the train which she could see from their kitchen window, she knew it was 1.30, time to open the shop.

The first misdemeanour of these pupils to be reported was in 1879 when a group of boys fixed a parcel of chemicals to the rails in the tunnel, where it exploded under the wheels of a train. The driver pulled up in a hurry, causing consternation in the carriages. The culprits were paraded in front of a G.W.R. representative who administered a stern lecture. At later dates it became a 'dare' for boys to put a halfpenny on a rail in the tunnel before a train came, then wait in a 'refuge' until it had gone by. Then, with luck, they would retrieve the flattened coin as a trophy.

Pupils at the Blue School, Wells, also used the line. Bunty Tracy, one of their scholars resident in Winscombe, who later became a trustee of the Railway Walk Society, remembers travelling with her brother and sister. When they went home at the end of the school day, the stationmaster at Wells, at the request of the head teachers, saw that the boys and the girls were in separate compartments before the train left. In those days, of course, there were no corridors. Naturally, at the next stop, Wookey Hole, they rearranged themselves.

The affectionate memories travellers still have are perhaps due to the general friendliness of the staff, helping to load or unload bicycles in the guard's van, or watching to see if anyone was running, puffing and panting up the incline, before they blew the whistle.

Decline and Closure

Once the stone haulage for the Blagdon Reservoir construction was completed, the Wrington Vale Light Railway had far less success than the Cheddar Valley route, and in 1931 ordinary passenger traffic stopped. Freight continued, but the Wrington to Blagdon section closed to traffic in 1950 apart from occasional 'specials', and the rails were taken up on this part in 1952. Freight trains, especially coal, continued to run from Congresbury to Wrington for another 11 years.

During the 1950's, people and goods increasingly went by road, and traffic of all types diminished on the Yatton to

Cheddar line, with passenger trains being progressively replaced by single diesel coaches which themselves became less and less frequent. Although in the bad winter of 1962, people went by train on this line when the roads were almost impassable, British Rail followed the recommendations of the Beeching Report and discontinued all normal passenger and freight trains in 1963. A final train, very full with mourning or interested passengers ran on September 7th, 1963, and the rails and sleepers carried were away by the very last train of all in 1964. This is the only one that one of the authors (A.B.) saw.

Freight, especially stone, continued to run from Cheddar to Witham junction till March 28th 1969, and stone is still carried (1998) from Merehead Quarry, the other side of Wells. Further along the same line, at Cranmore, the East Somerset Railway runs private steam trains, and is well worth a visit.

16

2 FROM RAILWAY TO WALKWAY AND CYCLEWAY

The Campaign

Inhabitants of villages on or near the abandoned track found that it made a pleasant walk which did not get muddy in wet weather. Technically of course they were trespassing, but neither British Rail nor anyone else seemed to worry about this. In Winscombe, where the modern village had largely grown up around the railway station, shoppers also found the track a safe and convenient way from one part of the village to another.

The first attempts to legalise walking on any part of the track were in 1976, when a few residents of The Grove in Winscombe approached British Rail via the Parish Council to ask that the short length of track between their road and the Primary School could be used as a safe walk to school by local children. This move disappeared without trace, and only when British Rail leased bits of track to land users bordering the line did the excitement start.

Barriers appeared here and there, obstructing the track and interfering with walks that people were by then taking for granted. Walkers simply stepped over the netting put up to mark out grazing areas for goats, but high fences put up by

Opposite top: Towards Congresbury from Yatton, 1964;
Opposite Centre: Near Congresbury, 1983;
Opposite bottom: Pupils riding under Fiveways Bridge on their way home on the Axbridge - Cheddar Cycleway, c. 1990. Note loading platform on right.

17

residents on the west side of The Grove to protect their leased garden extensions totally closed the route. Our group of outraged inhabitants formed an Action Group to find out what was happening and what could be done about it. We sent letters to British Rail and the Parish Council in July 1977, and by November had collected 727 signatures for a petition to lease from British Rail the part of the track in our Parish as a walk and nature reserve.

On February 20th, 1978, what we then called the "Winscombe Parish Council Railway Walk Committee" held its Inaugural Meeting, and by March the proposals had been circulated to all relevant public bodies, and local meetings had been held. The original proposal was only for the stretch from Shute Shelve to Sandford, but with the encouragement of the Countryside Commission, we extended our ambitions northwards to Yatton and southwards to Cheddar, and renamed ourselves "The Cheddar Valley Railway Walk Society".

Early in 1979, British Rail decided to sell the line, completely changing the rules of the game, so we now had to persuade the District Council to buy the line on our behalf. In the same year Cyclebag approached us with the idea of making the route into a cycleway/walkway as they had done with some other derelict railways. After initial hesitation we accepted this idea of a joint project, and Cyclebag prepared a detailed scheme from Yatton to Cheddar.

When the opponents of the Walk realised that it was not just a pipe dream of a few starry-eyed cranks, but that it might really come into existence, more open hostility emerged. The most formidable opposition came from the farmers in the flat land bordering the northern part of the line, and especially those at Congresbury. They had good reason for wanting to own the railway land bordering and sometimes between their fields, and had believed that if the line closed they could buy back the land that their predecessors had sold to the Railway Company. They now felt cheated by suggestions that it should be offered to somebody else first. Other conspicuous opponents were residents of the west side of The Grove, who were determined to buy their garden extensions and disliked the idea of a public footpath past the end of their back gardens. In August 1980 the Council approved our planning application for a Leisure Walk, so from then on, the Railway Walk was accepted in principle as Council policy. In January 1981, British Rail finally produced their offer to the Council to sell what was left of the branch line within Woodpring District, excluding the station sites, but guaranteeing a right-of-way through.

At a tense meeting on 17 November 1981, the Council agreed in principle to purchase the land for a leisure walk, but only after the cycling part of the proposal had been dropped. The purchase was completed in April 1983, including a further short stretch of the line from the tunnel to the A38, although this was in another district, Sedgemoor, and another county, Somerset. The route was then complete from Yatton to the A38 at Shute Shelve, apart from one serious gap.

Establishing the Walk

Our job now was to make the Walk walkable and find the money to do this. We got confirmation of the grants which had been more or less promised, increased our subscription, and held fund-raising events in villages all along the line.

The main tasks facing us were fencing the route, clearing bramble and other obstructions, improving drainage and providing access points. Manpower Services trainees and local volunteers were our two sources of labour. The Manpower Services trainees (16-17 year old youths on a one-year training scheme) were one of our sources of labour. The other helpers were volunteers, people of all ages, usually local residents who enjoyed walking the line, perhaps with their dogs, who were willing to spend a Saturday afternoon or occasionally an evening helping the Walk, and local Scout groups.

Now that we knew our boundaries, we did our best to deal with attempted annexations by some bordering land users,

Above: Fences go up behind The Grove.

Below: Fences courtesy of Manpower Services.

though only the Council had legal authority over the land. As the essential work neared completion, we had to repair fences which had been vandalised and organise a wardening system to try to prevent damage and misuse of the line, particularly the incursion of young motorcyclists. We also found time for signposting and preparation of leaflets to help users of the Walk, and to encourage walking and conservation groups in the area to organise walks on the line. Our success so far was recognised by Avon Community Council, who judged us the Village Venture Award winners for 1983/4.

Maintaining the Walk

Shute Shelve, Winscombe and Sandford

Around Winscombe, where the idea of the Walk originated, we had a great deal of support and little hostility, our main task being controlling the vegetation, especially bramble. On the dry embankment on Shute Shelve south of the tunnel we were asked by the Ministry of Agriculture to control two agricultural pests on our land. One was rabbits, which find the bramble-covered embankments alongside pasture ideal for breeding. The other pest was ragwort, which grows profusely on railway tracks, and in hay is poisonous to livestock, particularly horses. The plants should be pulled up before they set seed which otherwise spreads over the surrounding pasture.

Our local volunteers with secateurs and slashers, Scout groups, parties of scholars from local schools, and Community Service groups did most of the work controlling vegetation, though we employed contractors occasionally for major scrub clearance.

Two improvement tasks for which outside contractors were necessary were surfacing and drainage. The coarse chippings used by the railway were not an ideal surface for walking, so we had the trackway progressively covered with fine crushed limestone through most of the Winscombe stretch, giving a much pleasanter surface, the cost being met by appeals to members. We also had a major drainage problem by Winscombe Recreation Ground, where increased land drainage caused flooding across the line after heavy rain.

Vandalism in this area was not too serious, and was mainly damage to barriers, which were repaired by a local contractor. More worrying were 'rave' parties in the tunnel - massive dances going on all night and sometimes for an entire holiday weekend. This upset local residents and the farmer whose field had been used as a car park and we were left with many sacks of bottles and cans to dispose of. All we could do was to make the access for the ravers and their equipment as inconvenient as possible and hope that the increase in legal sites and changes in fashion would make raves on our land less frequent.

Congresbury and Yatton

Congresbury had two problems not present anywhere else. The first was the 'Sandford Gap', where British Rail had sold about half a mile of the track to two Sandford farmers before the Railway Walk Society came into existence. As there was no way of by-passing this private land, it made the one and a half miles of the Walk into a cul-de-sac.

The other Congresbury problem was horses on the line. As the route passes through nearly 10 miles of countryside where the main industry until recently had been livestock farming, we were not surprised to have to deal with the unwanted presence on the track of farm animals, which have included cattle, sheep, horses and, at one stage, pigs. Even so, these incursions were usually dealt with fairly quickly and amicably, but the Congresbury horse problem was very different.

Before the District Council purchased the railway land, horses had been reported grazing on the line between Sandford and Congresbury. The horses were said locally to be owned by the Penfolds, a long-established family of travellers, but when the Council established which member of the family owned the animals, he claimed that they were lawfully there by right-of-use. This claim was disputed by the Council, which started proceedings to exclude the horses from the Walk.

The Congresbury members complained bitterly that they or their friends found the horses frightening, while the Society found the situation frustrating as we had no legal authority over the land. The local farmers also noticed the apparent impotence of the Society and the Council, and some of them felt free to allow their livestock to roam on the line. With no sign of any solution to their problems, these formerly enthusiastic members became discouraged.

The legal case was not straightforward. In a claim of right-of-way it is necessary to demonstrate undisputed use for 20 years, but in a claim for land use by grazing animals the period is only 12 years. The period claimed was largely after the line had been closed, but while it was still owned by British Rail, who by then had discarded any relevant documents. In the end the Council came to an agreement allowing the grazing rights on part of the Congresbury section, subject to walkers' right of passage and various restrictions to limit the damage to the surface and vegetation. This was drawn up in 1994 and signed in June 1995.

Things went better in the northern half of the Congresbury section and at Yatton. The line was well used by walkers near the two villages, both of which had ponds close to their access points. With the help of the Avon Wildlife Trust, Tony and Faith Moulin in Yatton, and Pip Nabb and Ken Blake in Congresbury, members with a keen interest in wildlife, formed 'Watch' groups (junior Wildlife Trust branches), which used these ponds as centres for their activities. The national 'Pondwatch' series being screened on television at the time helped to generate and maintain interest. Watch parties cleared the Congresbury pond and extensive reed beds of dumped tyres and other hardware. The Yatton pond did not have extensive reed beds, but was deep, making it suitable for toads to breed, so by co-operating, the two groups could organise

23

very varied activities.

While the Congresbury pond was on the privately owned station site, the one at Yatton was on Railway Walk land. Tony and Faith Moulin therefore put their efforts into developing the Yatton pond, which went on to be the the Wildfowl and Wetlands Trust 'Wildlife Pond of the Year' for 1991. Advisors from the Avon Wildlife Trust had been fascinated by what they found, not only in the pond, but also in the surrounding network of rhynes, and had suggested that the area was worth environmental protection. Representatives of English Nature surveyed the pond and some of the rhynes in 1991, reporting a rich variety of plant and invertebrate species, both in the water and on the banks. As a result of their report, the area, known as the 'Wemberham Triangle' was notified as a Site of Special Scientific Interest (SSSI) in 1994. Philip Tolerton, one of the advisors who had been helping the Moulins, was convinced that the Cheddar Valley Railway Walk was a valuable but under-used asset, and in due course was able to explore its possibilities. This led to the whole length of line owned by the Council being declared a Local Nature Reserve in 1996/97.

The Axbridge-Cheddar Cycleway

Once the Woodspring part of the Walk was established, we tried to help the few of our members resident in Axbridge and Cheddar to extend the route into their area, at first without success. Then a near fatal accident to an Axbridge pupil cycling to school at Cheddar caused the Head to take action, leading a group of concerned parents along the old railway track as a possible safe cycling route. When the schools and the PTA's backed the idea, it took off. Planning permission for a cycle and walkway was granted in March 1986, and a year later Sedgemoor District Council bought the required land from British Rail.

Developments since the railway closed necessitated several diversions, with the Cycleway descending from the Axbridge by-pass, which had taken over part of the old line, and finishing near the old Cheddar Station, now a listed building. As soon as the Cycleway Group got planning permission, they started raising funds, but only when work started on the first section did money really come in.

The access point on the by-pass was opposite the entrance to the St Michaels Cheshire Homes. David Hassall, one of their residents helped them to put their considerable fund-raising expertise at the disposal of the Cycleway Group, who in turn took care to see that the barriers chosen to keep out motorcycles could be negotiated by their wheelchairs.

Working parties with strimmers, slashers and secateurs cleared the vegetation ahead of the surfacing contractors, doing the clearing by hand, not just to keep down cost but to disturb the wildlife as little as possible. Volunteers also helped in designing and construction, planting and preparing information, the work reaching its climax with the official opening on October 21st, 1990. The Cycleway Group then organised volunteer wardens to report damage and other problems, and continued with working parties to keep the path clear.

The horse problem at Congresbury.

25

Cycling all the Way

The Vision

Phil Tolerton, when he became part-time Countryside Officer to Woodspring District Council, envisaged a possible network of routes for walkers, wheelchair users, cyclists and, in places, horseriders, partly along old railways. The easiest part of this jigsaw to put in place seemed to be the Cheddar Valley Railway, where all that was needed was to close the gap at Sandford and convert the rest of the Walk to a cycleway.

After explaining his ideas to us, Phil commissioned a study of the practicability and desirability of converting the Walk to a cycleway. The report, by 'Landmark', a Bristol environmental group, suggested that a continuous walking and cycling route from Yatton to Shute Shelve was desirable and should be achievable. A parallel horseriding track on the Congresbury section within the former railway land was also considered a possible option. We then sent a questionnaire to all members of the Society who overwhelmingly supported the main recommendations. In the Summer of 1996, North Somerset Council, (replacement for the old Woodspring District Council), approved the report, so from then on it was Council policy to create a cycleway along the old Cheddar Valley Railway, as and when resources permitted.

The Start

The short length of line at Shute Shelve between the A38 and the lay-by on the Axbridge by-pass came on the market in two separate bits ten years apart, and each time we appealed to our members and bought the land. The final purchase gave us continuity from Sandford to the Axbridge lay-by. This interested Andrew Combes, the Somerset County Cycling Officer, who had been keen to join our Walk to the network of cycling and wheelchair routes he was building up around the Somerset Levels. Andrew and Philip then prepared a joint project for a cycleway/walkway along the old railway track to connect the lay-by on the by-pass with Winscombe, and they put this to their respective county councils, with our support. Work started in the Spring of 1997. Somerset County were responsible for the cost and management of the work within their county, that is from the Axbridge lay-by to the southern end of the tunnel, Andrew Combes being in charge of this team which started work at the lay-by. Where the railway originally crossed the A38 over a bridge long since demolished, they sloped the path down from the railway track to the pavement and erected an elaborate system of barriers and islands to make the crossing as safe as possible. At the tunnel, Paul Paton, the North Somerset Cycling and Footpath Officer took over, continuing through the tunnel to Winscombe Recreation Ground. On June 10th 1997, Paul, Andrew and Philip organised a tape-cutting ceremony at the county boundary at the southern end of the tunnel, with the Press from both counties present, to inaugurate a route which soon proved popular.

Continuity at Last !

Yatton Station

When Woodspring District Council bought the bulk of the Cheddar Valley line for the Railway Walk, British Rail did not permit access to the Walk from the station site. This meant that anyone coming from the station had to walk a mile along public highways, among local and through traffic, to reach the Walk. It also made the northern quarter of a mile of the Walk into a cul-de-sac. Over the years, we and the Council tried to persuade British Rail to allow a way through, but without success.

After privatisation these attempts were renewed, but nobody then seemed to know who actually owned the land. Suddenly, in September 1997, Railway Properties Limited, a company that nobody had heard of before, advertised for sale by auction a number of railway yards and other properties, including much of Yatton Station site. With only a few weeks available, Tony Moulin gathered support from sympathisers to persuade Railway Properties to withdraw the land from auction. A consortium including North Somerset Council, YANSEC (which collects the local landfill tax), Sustrans, Yatton Parish Council, and local environmental groups (including us), raised the money to cover the purchase and necessary work. A celebratory function was held at the Railway Inn, Yatton, followed by a tour of the new acquisition, on February 20th, 1998, the 20th anniversary of the formal inauguration of the Railway Walk Society.

This land, which could justifiably be a nature reserve in its own right, and especially valuable for migrant redwings and fieldfares, has now been incorporated in the Local Nature Reserve. Early in 1999 local volunteers cleared the track and a surface was laid suitable for walking and, when appropriate, cycling.

The 'Sandford Gap'

The sale by British Rail of a section of the line in Sandford to two local farmers before the Railway Walk Society came into existence had, from the beginning, caused the greatest weakness in the Railway Walk project. Because of the absence of public footpaths crossing the line south of Congresbury, there was no satisfactory way of by-passing this half-mile or so of private land. This divided the Walk into two quite unconnected parts and meant that the one and a half miles from Congresbury was another cul-de-sac.

From the moment of purchase of the railway land by Woodspring, the Council and the Society tried without success to negotiate a way through or round this private land to give continuity to the Walk. Then, in 1998, Phil Tolerton was able to agree a route with John Thatcher, one of the landowners, for a permissive footpath through his land, so that for the first time, a Walk from Yatton to Cheddar became possible.

Winscombe Station

British Rail, when they sold the line to the Council, did not include Winscombe Station, but guaranteed a pedestrian right-of-way through, selling the site later to a property company. In 1997, a group of Winscombe residents made a successful bid for lottery money to help to buy the site and convert it into a Millennium Village Green. This was supported by Winscombe & Sandford Parish Council, the Railway Walk Society, the Local History Society and other local groups and individuals.

Work on this project officially began on February 27th, 1999, when the 'First Sod' was cut by Mrs Gunn using the ceremonial spade which her great grandmother, Mrs Yatman had used 132 years earlier to inaugurate work on the Cheddar Valley Railway. This creation of the the Village Green will make the management of the route through the quarter mile of the station site easier, will permit the continuation of a cycleway through it, and provide a good starting point for the Winscombe walks.

Shute Shelve purchase.

29

3 SURVIVING RAILWAY FEATURES
OF THE WALK

We can recognise old railways by several characteristic features: bridges, embankments, cuttings, railposts, railway hotels, workers' buildings and, if all else fails, 'Station Road'.

Bridges over Roads

Built to be lasting, acclaimed as the best,
Were the bridges that carried the trains to the West.
The one in our village was still looking fine
Long after Lord Beeching had shut down the line.

It carried a footpath where walkers could go
Safe from the cars and the lorries below,
But highways departments were paid for improving
The way that the traffic on wheels kept moving.

The bridge was a blockage, slowed everything down
To the speed you would find in the thick of a town,
While the headroom, which caught their professional eye
Couldn't take trucks over four metres high.

When builders bought acres of neighbouring land,
A glorious weapon was put in their hand.
"The traffic will double, the builder must pay
To get this obstruction right out of the way."

Down through the village, the high street, the lanes,
The bridge was now raising more steam than the trains.
In Council, on doorsteps, in car park or walk,
We argued its fate in a torrent of talk.

31

"It upsets the traffic, reduces its pace!"
"That cuts out the speeding - please leave it in place!"
"The headroom's too low!" - while the locals reply:
"We don't want the trucks over four metres high!"

All of us righteously called to our aid
Safety and beauty, tradition and trade,
But were sure it would be on the question of cost
That the war would be won, or the war would be lost.

We knew that decisions about our backyard
Were made in the city - that came very hard -
As hard as conceding to others the right
To root for their corner and put up a fight.

They said it would finish as everything must -
Ashes to ashes and dust to dust.
The headroom, then reaching right up to the sky
Would be great - for the trucks over four metres high.

But, just as the shoppers were fearing the worst,
The highways department abruptly reversed!
In village or town, they decided at last,
The cars and the lorries should not go too fast.

To match the new thinking, the bridge was to stay,
With bollards to guard a pedestrian way.
Incoming drivers must wait at the line
Heeding, we hoped, the priority sign.

So the landmark erected to carry a train
Is safe - until policy changes again.
A beauty? An eyesore? A blessing? A block?
The bridge is still standing as firm as a rock!

The Fox brothers used the same simple and attractive design
for all the bridges along the line, so whether the railway went
over or under, whether it was a major or minor road, a farm

track or a stream, the bridges differed only in size and in the nature of the footings. While the same Mendip Dolomitic Conglomerate was also used in other structures along the line, it is on the bridges that this stonework can be particularly easily examined today. For example, if we look carefully at the surviving bridges we can usually find marks of the drill holes used for splitting the stones.

The solidity of construction meant that the bridges could continue to fulfil serve their original purpose with very little maintenance for as long as that purpose existed, and would be expensive to knock down. For this reason, most of them have survived, only those considered to be very much in the way being demolished.

Bridges over roads got in the way of road widening schemes, so only one has survived, and that almost by chance. There were three between Yatton and Cheddar, those over the Weston-super-Mare - Bath Road (A368) at Sandford, the Weston-super-Mare - Wells Road (A371) at Winscombe and the Bristol - Taunton Road (A38) at Shute Shelve. Somerset County Council Highways Department, the authority for all the roads in the area at the time of closure, was anxious to demolish all these bridges, so that the roads could be widened. This they did at Sandford and Shute shelve with very little comment. The Sandford demolition they had planned to show to the World. The press and television were invited, the bridge was fitted with detonators and explosive charges, the road closed, and with the cameras set up at a safe distance and everybody warned, the charges were fired. There was a great bang, and slowly the smoke and the dust cleared. The bridge was completely unmoved! The contractors had underestimated the solidity of the work of the engineers of the 1860's. A day or two later they installed a heavier charge and then, without the presence of the press and television cameras, the bridge finally gave in.

The bridge over Woodborough Road at Winscombe was quite another story. It was surrounded by houses, being in the centre of the village, which had really grown up around the station next to the bridge. This made the demolition trickier. Nevertheless a date and time were fixed, the village notified and the bridge drilled for explosive charges. On the appointed day at the appointed time the village listened - but there was not even a bang! The contractor had gone into liquidation and the receivers had taken over on the very day planned for the demolition.

Before a new contractor had been appointed, somebody came up with a project to use this part of the line for moving quarry stone, so British Rail decided to keep the bridge for the time being. The quarry stone idea came to nothing, but in the meantime local government had been reorganised. The part of Somerset containing Winscombe had been transferred to the newly invented County of Avon, which became the authority for highways and stategic planning, while local planning became the responsibility of the equally new District of Woodspring. One of the things the reorganisation produced most effectively was delay. Avon took over the roadworks programmes for Bristol and all the areas it inherited from Somerset and Gloucestershire, and had to match these to its budget. In deciding which items were most urgent, the country areas, of course, believed it gave the greatest priority to Bristol.

Before the County of Avon had put road widening at Winscombe anywhere near the top of its agenda, two things had happened. One was a planning application to build a large housing estate, and the other was the creation of the Railway Walk incorporating the bridge, which would separate the proposed housing estate from the village centre. Conflict came slowly but surely. The Avon highways department opposed the housing development because the residents of the proposed estate would have to go under the bridge to reach the village shops, along a road that was barely wide enough for two-way traffic, let alone a pavement. They would lift their objection to the proposed estate only when the bridge had been demolished and the road widened to provide a pavement.

The Railway Walk Society was very upset at the idea of knocking down the bridge, which would leave a gap in the Walk, with the users having to come down to cross a busy road. In opposing the demolition, the Society had support from many villagers, because the bridge slowed down through traffic entering the shopping centre. We prepared plans for archways through the railway embankment to let residents of the proposed new estate reach the shops, but nothing other than complete removal of the bridge was acceptable to Avon Highways Department.

Woodspring District Council, caught between the bridge supporters on the one hand and the developer and the County Council on the other, looked for a way out. The Council were well placed to negotiate with the developer, as they owned the bridge, having bought it along with the rest of the line, and were also the planning authority for the area. They struck a deal by which the developer, Mr Smith, was to pay the cost of demolishing the bridge, and in addition, for the destruction of this amenity, he was required to pay £70,000 compensation, which the Council could then use to build a replacement footbridge wide and high enough to satisfy Avon County Highways Department.

This, the Council thought, would satisfy everybody, but it horrified the Railway Walk Committee, as there was no allowance for inflation. The Council officers were used to developers who wanted to start as soon as possible to get some return on their outlay, but we knew that this local builder always took his time and was likely to sit on this plot for many years, while the cost of a replacement footbridge would escalate.

It became increasingly clear that the compensation would not cover the cost of the footbridge and that the Council had no intention of meeting the difference. The Society registered a Land Charge on the Railway Walk land (including the bridge), which it had agreed to lease from the Council. This, if enforceable, would mean that the status of this property could not be changed without the society's consent. As a lease had not actually been signed, the Council insisted that our action was invalid and unlawful, and demanded that we rescind it, which we were willing to do only if we had an assurance about a replacement footbridge. The builder naturally refused to go ahead with his development until the legal complications were resolved. The result was deadlock, with the Council becoming increasingly angry. While the Society and the Council remained at loggerheads, we were unable to deal effectively with trespass anywhere on the line, producing problems which were more difficult to tackle later.

When the housing boom faded, the pressure to develop relaxed, tempers cooled and normal relations with the Council resumed. With plans for a Winscombe by-pass being more seriously discussed, Mr Smith now saw the possibility that the bridge might be allowed to stay. He could then build his houses without extra cost to himself or offence to the supporters of the bridge. He did not have to wait for the by-pass. Attitudes to traffic changed both nationally and locally, 'traffic calming' being the new philosophy. The bridge was now an asset, slowing down vehicles as they entered the shopping area. As the width under the bridge was insufficient for both two-way traffic and pavements, a one-way system was installed with priority to the outgoing traffic. On each side of the roadway was a narrow pavement protected by bollards. The most surprising thing about this arrangement was that the head-on collisions predicted when it was first installed did not happen.

Bridges over the Line

Of the original bridges over the line, only the northernmost, which lifted the Bristol - Weston-super-Mare road (A370) over the railway at Congresbury, has gone. It was demolished soon after closure, and the road widened.

Going southwards, we come to the Droveway Bridge which carries the Sandford - Puxton road (Nye Road) at Sandford.

The land under the bridge is privately owned and, at the moment of writing, the Walk does not exist there, and the bridge can only be seen from the road. Continuing south, we reach two bridges fairly close together in the wooded cutting between Sandford and Winscombe. Both carry lanes, the first of which is a private track within a farm and the second, Ilex Lane, a roadway to the Cemetery.

The next bridge over the line, about 400 yards south of the site of Winscombe Station, carries the Lynch, a residential road within the village. Finally, on the edge of Cheddar, the road to Wedmore goes over the busy Fiveways Bridge. There is good access to examine both these bridges from above and below.

Accomodation Bridges

Accomodation bridges, or cattle creeps, allowed farm animals to move under the railway between fields on opposite sides of an embankment, and were usually built where the line divided a pre-existing farm. The two such bridges on the line between Yatton and Cheddar have both survived and are easily seen. One is in Winscombe village with the back gardens of the Homefield Close estate on one side and a step-down transformer in a field on the other. At present it is used by the electricity supply company for access.

The other accomodation bridge, about half-way between the tunnel and the A38 crossing is still available for its original purpose. As the line is on a high embankment in open grassland, it is an impressive landmark visible from footpaths in the surrounding countryside.

Bridges over Waterways

The Fox Brothers' Bristol & Exeter team had to lay the line across land with a variety of rivers, streams and drainage ditches and to ensure that the water flow was not obstructed. The largest of these waterways was the Congresbury Yeo, where they built a substantial bridge to carry the line across the river. Unfortunately, when the line was closed the Drainage

Board had it demolished to make it easier to dredge the river. All along the line, with the exception of the dry hillside south of the tunnel, the Railway Company cut drainage ditches along both sides of the track with facilities at intervals for the water to pass from one side to the other. In places it was sufficient to have a pipe under the line, but in the flat land between Yatton and Sandford where the ditches along the line are connected with the field drainage rhynes, something more was needed, and altogether they built some 20 culverts of varying sizes under the line between Yatton station and Sandford. These are effectively small bridges, wide and deep enough to take a considerable flow of water, and are built of brick with a conspicuous parapet. Most are in good condition, but some have been damaged by the heavy equipment currently used for dredging the rhynes.

Where the railway went through the Mendips, the engineers built several bridges over streams. The most northerly of these, between Sandford Station and Ilex Lane, bridges Towerhead Brook, crossing from east to west on its way to the Banwell River running through the levels north of the Mendips. Just south of the back gardens of The Grove in Winscombe, a similar small bridge goes over the bed of what was the infant Lox Yeo River. This also crosses east to west, but then goes south-west, to join the Axe flowing along the southern side of the Mendips. The stream which went under the railway here is now dry, and the culvert is currently overgrown and easily missed.

On the Axbridge-Cheddar Cycleway, about 300 yards from the by-pass is a more impressive bridge over a stream. The track is raised high above the Ellenge Stream which then continues north of the reservoir, past the sewage works into the rhyne system of the levels draining through the Cheddar Yeo and the Axe.

The platform at Winscombe Station.

Left: Broad gauge rails used for fencing, Axbridge Station.

Below: The Railway Inn at Sandford.

Stations

The stations were all typical in design and construction of the work of the Fox Brothers, the Bristol & Exeter engineers. They had the same blockwork of Mendip conglomerate stone and chalet style roofs with characteristc bargeboards and orange tiles, but differed in size and complexity, depending on their importance.

Yatton Station is, of course, still in use, and the buildings at Sandford and Axbridge have survived, as has a substantial part of the larger station at Cheddar, but those at Congresbury and Winscombe were demolished a few years after closure, for reasons which are not very obvious

Yatton Station was originally a triple junction, with the main line, the Clevedon line and the Cheddar Valley line, but is now only a main line station. The signal boxes were removed after closure of the branch lines, but the Great Western seats have survived.

The former Sandford & Banwell Station, the most accessible to the public, now houses the Sandford Stone Centre, the station and accessory buildings being very well preserved and painted in Great Western colours. Garden ornaments now wait on what was both the 'up' and the 'down' platform. The passing loop was intended for goods traffic only, most goods from this side of Wells being headed for Bristol or, if milk, for London. A little south of the station site at Sandford was a shunting yard connected to private rail from Sandford Quarry, where stone was loaded directly into trucks to be taken to destinations nationwide. Part of the route where this quarry track curved round towards the shunting yard can still be traced

Axbridge Station, now alongside the by-pass, is used as a youth centre, while the shunting yard is a children's playground. The station building, together with with the old engine sheds, is best seen from the verge on the other side of the by-pass road.

The very grand station at Cheddar was partly demolished

41

when the line was closed. A stone-working company, specialising in church and cathedral restorations, uses the listed surviving part of the building, together with the former shunting yards. A very imposing stationmaster's house stands alongside the station.

Station Sites

In 1995, Arthur Westcott, a retired stationmaster (1954-1963), still lived in the Congresbury stationmaster's house, the only surviving building on this station site. It is not the original Bristol & Exeter house, but was built in 1933 by the Great Western Railway, having been designed by Jack Dunster and James Burnett. As at the other sites where the station building has been demolished, the platforms have survived, more or less. The 'down' platform was built by the Bristol & Exeter, and the 'up' platform later by the Great Western when Congresbury became the junction for the Wrington Vale Light Railway, constructed over the period 1898-1901. A short stretch of the light railway can still be followed on the Walk. It starts to diverge to the left of the Cheddar Valley line about 300 yards south of the station, just within the privately owned station site. Both lines then enter Railway Walk land, gradually diverging for about 200 yards, after which the Wrington Vale track enters private land where it can still be seen for some distance curving away to the left. In the area on the Walk between the two tracks, there are a number of concrete sleepers. These were widely used during and just after the Second World War and were each for one rail only, set in pairs with steel stretcher bars between them to keep the correct distance between the rails.

At Winscombe the platform still has iron spear fencing, while the concrete standard of the Tilley-Challow oil lamp remains, together with most of the small windlass and pulley for hoisting and lowering. A jumble of orange-red and dark blue G.W.R. bricks indicates the former position of the station itself.

42

Station gardens were keenly maintained, often with crystal rocks marking the borders. Shrubs such as buddleia and cotoneaster, naturalised on all station sites, are frequently descendants of the station garden decor.

The Tunnel

As it was the biggest challenge to the builders of the line, they chose it for the ceremonial start to the whole operation, and it is still the most striking feature.

The tunnel is 180 yards long. From the north it is approached through a narrow cutting in the Keuper Marl, which tends to fall on to the track and particularly into the ditches alongside, causing drainage problems. The visitor then enters the tunnel itself through an arch in a massive stone wall, the entance and the wall having a similar appearance to the bridges all along the line except that the arch is elliptical, being higher than it is wide, whereas the arches in the bridges are semi-circular. Because of the clay soil, the northern part of the tunnel is lined with stone or brick. The vertical walls are lined with the same Dolomitic Conglomerate blocks as the entrance wall, with 'refuges' built into them at intervals for line workmen to slip into when trains were passing. The arched ceiling consist of large bricks laid lengthwise along the tunnel and now blackened by nearly a century of smoke. Water drips down between the bricks and stone blocks along the whole length of this part of the tunnel.

A little over half-way through, there is a striking change. Beyond this point the excavation was through hard rock which gave a self-supporting roof needing no lining. At the junction of the lined and unlined regions water drips and runs down the walls more freely than anywhere else in the tunnel and a large stalactite-like column has formed on the west wall. This is one of the limestone formations described more fully in Chapter 5. It has a glossy white surface containing dark spots which are the remains of insects which have become entombed in the growing limestone surface.

From here onwards the tunnel is higher, wider and much drier than elsewhere. The occasional patches of limestone deposited since the tunnel was built are softer than true cave stalactites and are often coloured red with iron. Those on the ceiling are mostly 'straw stalactites' - thin tubes which break off as soon as their weight is too much for their frail stems. The rock formations can be seen very well, with different strata running obliquely up the walls and across the roof. Apart from the alternate layers of limestone and shale of different thicknesses and different colours, the visitor can easily find drill marks in the rock walls showing the working of the tunnellers a century ago.

On some very cold mornings the drips themselves may be frozen to give a 'fairy cave' appearance with stalactites of ice. Under all conditions it is worth while to take a torch to examine the features of the tunnel more closely, though the strata and the working of the rock continue for some distance along the cutting.

The coarse limestone chippings on the track bed were covered in 1991 with crushed limestone to give a better walking surface. This, in turn, was covered with tarmac in 1997 when this part of the Walk became a cycleway, to give a surface which would stand up to the constant dripping from the roof.

Other Surviving Railway Features

Loading platforms for limestone were built by the Railway Company at several places along the line, the best preserved being at Callow Rock near Fiveways Bridge in Cheddar (see page 16), where there is also an old rail acting as a barrier and fence post. Retaining walls are rare, but one, clothed in ferns, is still supporting the clay cutting north of the tunnel.

Simple huts for gangers were erected all along the line and the ruins of one of these, where the Walk was diverted near Sandford Station, were still visible in 1996. Another was recently swept away near Yatton when a rhyne was mechanically cleaned out. The navvies building the line also made huts for themselves and the remains of one of these can be seen in the undergrowth north of the tunnel.

When the Bristol & Exeter converted the line to standard gauge in 1875, they cut up the old rails to use as fencing posts, which can be found here and there all along the line. Old railway gates for farm crossings and wooden wicket gates are slowly disappearing, but worth looking for. Old railway wagons linger in fields and gardens. One is slowly decaying in a field west of the Sandford cutting. Some of the remaining wooden sleepers are still about but tend to move and then disappear. Railway workers could have allotments by the track, especially near stations, and raspberries can still be seen on some of these plots.

Every station had its 'Station Hotel', but most changed their name after the line closed. Among the few keeping the connection are a 'Railway Inn' at Yatton and another at Sandford. The signal visible to passing motorists at the one at Sandford is an old G.W.R. square post signal of a type that was steadily replaced from the mid-thirties onwards, and will have been one of the two 'starters'. The 'Strawberry Special' at Draycott which is further along the line than the present Railway Walk, has many pictures and photographs of the old railway. For anyone interested in railways, all these inns are worth a visit.

While any individual feature such as an embankment, a cutting, a bridge or a railway-type building, will in itself suggest a railway, it is the presence of a number of these features one after another that tells even someone who is not a railway buff, that here was once a railway. Looking out for these surviving bits of history can make a stroll along the Walk much more interesting.

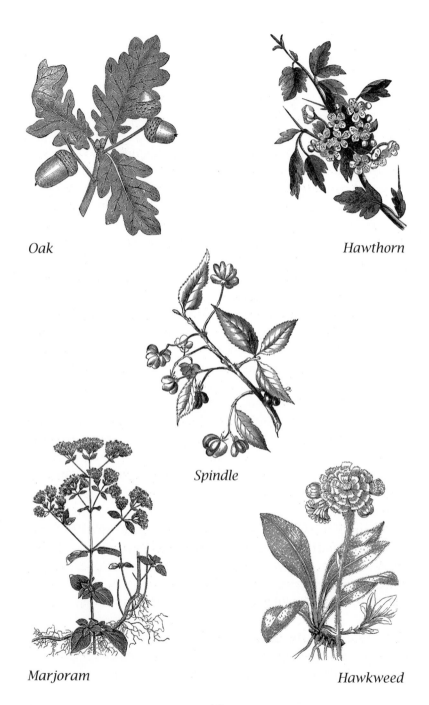

Oak

Hawthorn

Spindle

Marjoram

Hawkweed

4 PLANTS AND ANIMALS

Based on the various reports and studies published, we will describe the dominant features of the flora and fauna of the line as a whole, and then the characteristic, and any specially interesting aspects of the various sections along the route. While this should give a good indication of nature of these habitats, it is not an attempt to list the species present.

In 1995 Ingle, studying the flora of the Cheddar Valley Railway Walk, found a general similarity to what had been reported on other railways, disused or operational. Various individuals and groups have looked at the ecology of the Cheddar Valley Railway Walk over the period 1978 to 1995, but each of these studies was for a specific and limited purpose and confined to just one section of the Walk. Nevertheless, between them they cover the whole length and give a great deal of information.

In 1997, North Somerset Council commissioned an ecological survey of the Walk from Yatton Station to Shute Shelve as guidance for the management of the Local Nature Reserve. This was carried out by the Avon Wildlife Trust in May, July and September of that year, and became available in February 1998.

Clearly, any change in the management of a particular section is likely to start a succession of changes in the flora and at least the invertebrate fauna, as happened when the Axbridge-Cheddar Cyleway was created. It will also occur in some of the older parts of the Walk which are being modified for cycling.

Features of the Line as a Whole
On the well-drained track bed of limestone chippings on a broken limestone hardcore, we find plants tolerant of both

47

alkaline conditions and drought. The plants on the track itself are almost identical along the whole route except where soil has fallen on to the gravel surface and where there is heavy shade, and, of course, where the Walk has been diverted and is no longer on the original track bed. Ragwort, some Hawkweeds and a few grasses are the most conspicuous residents. Similar flora will also be found at all the station sites, together with Buddleia and Cotoneasters, which were often initially planted to adorn the station, and other typical colonisers of derelict land, such as Rose-bay Willowherb, Marjoram, Common Toadflax and Wild Carrot.

On the edge of the track, except where it is very shaded, are Field Bindweed, Birdsfoot Trefoil and coarser grasses with Dandelion and other pasture plants. These spread on to the track in the damper stretches and retreat further from it in the drier ones. Behind this, growing profusely and spreading on to the track wherever it is not cut back, is Bramble.

The hedgerows are predominantly Hawthorn, Blackthorn, Hazel, Dogwood and Dog Rose interwoven with Bramble, Great Bindweed (*Calystegia sepium*), Honeysuckle and Old Man's Beard (*Clematis vitalba*). The hedgerow trees are usually Ash, Oak (*Quercus robur*) and Sycamore with occasional Field Maple and Elder and the odd Spindle Tree, except in the wetlands, where the large trees are usually Grey Willow (*Salix cinerea*).

We find the commoner woodland, hedgerow and garden birds along the entire route in numbers varying according to the situation. There are noisy colonies of Rooks as well as Crows, Magpies and Starlings, while Kestrels, Buzzards, Tawny Owls and Little Owls hunt periodically over the line and the surrounding land. Songbirds include Blackbirds, Song and Mistle Thrushes, Chaffinches, Greenfinches, Bullfinches, Great Tits, Bluetits, Long-tailed Tits, Dunnocks, Robins, Wrens and, in winter, flocks of Fieldfares and Redwings. Badgers may be seen here and there, as may Foxes.

Throughout the Summer, Small White butterflies are conspicuous, and about as common are Small Tortoiseshell,

Peacock and Comma and, in late Summer, continental migrants such as Red Admirals with, in some years, Painted Ladies and Clouded Yellows. The non-use of herbicides and pesticides helps to give biodiversity, with the wide range of plants providing food for a variety of butterflies, including Red Admirals, whose furry black caterpillars can often be seen on the stinging nettles.

Yatton & Congresbury

The ponds, rhynes, damp verges and the surrounding moist pasture are a superb habitat for water-loving plants and animals. The drainage ditches (rhynes) which intersect the land connect with the ditches alongside the track which is on a slight embankment, the deep pond at Yatton and the shallower pond at Congresbury being part of this drainage system.

The Yatton section has done better for ecological studies than any other part of the line. Several limited surveys were carried out by the Avon Wildlife Trust between 1989 and 1994, and it was the location of Ingle's studies in 1995. In addition, the survey commissioned by North Somerset Council in 1997 was more thorough in this stretch than elsewhere. It is clearly species-rich. The local 'Watch' group, that is the junior branch of the Wildlife Trust, recording the plants actually in flower in the half mile from Biddle Street to Yatton Station over the period from May 20th to 23rd, 1991, found 46 species. Ingle in her prolonged study of plant distribution in the Yatton section recorded 65 species. It is impossible to say whether similar species numbers occur in areas which have not been investigated so fully, but comparison of the types of plants found shows very clearly the difference between this area and other parts of the route.

Ingle found the pattern of distribution across the track was very characteristic, and varied little from one location along it to another. This agrees with other observations in Yatton and those parts of the Congresbury section which have not been grazed by farm livestock. For most of the length there are four zones: the trackway, the verges, which are wide on the western side, the rhynes and the hedgerows.

The growth on the trackbed through the Yatton and Congresbury sections is more vigorous than elsewhere on the Walk, and contains more grass and more species. On the whole the same plants such as Ragwort and the hawkweeds are conspicuous, but those liking dry situations, such as Birdsfoot Trefoil and Marjoram, are rare here.

The verges have long lush grass together with Dandelions, Teazels, Saw-wort, Field Horsetail (*Equisetum arvense*) and other plants of neutral damp pasture. Drier patches may have Bramble and Hawthorn scrub, especially on the wider western side. The verges periodically receive the debris from dredging the rhynes, so the vegetation depends on whether, and how recently, the particular stretch has been covered. This will give stretches of tall ruderal (wasteland) grassland while it is recovering from the deposition material from rhyne clearing. The lower areas close to the rhynes have Tufted Hairgrass, Sedges (*Carex Sp.*) and reeds.

The rhynes, of course, are the reason for the special character of this region and why it earned the SSSI status described in Chapter 4. Above and below the waterline, flowering in succession, are Marsh Marigold, Yellow Flag, Bulrush, Hemlock Water Dropwort, Water Crowfoot, Frogbit, Common Reed (Phragmites australis) and Water Mint. Sedges and Common Reed are usual where the verges slope into the rhynes, together sometimes with Reed Sweetgrass (Phalaris arundinacea) and Great Sweetgrass (Glyceria maxima). On both sides of the River Yeo and the A370 at Congresbury are wide reed beds, the one west of the station site and connected to the pond being especially large.

In the hedgerows in most of this section, the largest trees are Grey Willows (*Salix cinerea*), with Alders being quite frequent, along with the usual Hawthorn and Blackthorn, though as the ground rises towards Sandford, there are increasing numbers of Ash and Oak . At the base of the hedges are Primroses and Lady's Smock.

The Weston-super-Mare Local Members Group of the RSPB have made surveys on and around the Yatton and Congresbury area of the Railway Walk each Winter and Spring from the end of 1994. While most of the birds seen elsewhere along the line are also found here, the most noticeable are those liking the rhynes and wet meadows. Moorhens swim and nest under the bushes at the edge of the pond at Yatton, while the rhynes have Herons fishing, and are visited by Teal and Water Rails. A few Cormorants are also about, both in Winter and Spring. The large reed bed at Congresbury is an important breeding site for Sedge Warblers, Reed Warblers and Reed Buntings. Kingfishers also inhabit this reed bed and other waterways in the area.

The large area of Blackthorn scrub, which was until recently part of the Yatton Station site, is a valuable winter feeding ground for migant Redwings and Fieldfares.

Many mammals find the Walk a useful corridor and hunting ground. In the rhynes, Mink have been seen and Water Shrews and also Water Voles, which are on the decrease nationally. On summer evenings, Noctule and Pipistrelle bats are around. Among reptiles, the wetlands favour Slow-worms and Grass Snakes, and the Adder may be seen in various sites adjacent to the Walk. Of the amphibians, Toads breed successfully in the deep pond at Yatton, while Common Frogs can breed in the shallower waters of the Congresbury pond and the rhynes, where the Smooth Newt has also been reported,

The 23 species of butterflies so far recorded on this stretch include the Orange Tip, a spreading colony of Marbled White and two colonies of Purple Hairstreak as well as the species common along the whole line. A range of species of dragonflies and damsel flies breed on the Yatton pond, and some also in the rhynes. On fine summer nights Crickets can be heard and Glow-worms (*Lampyris noctiluca*) seen in the grass along the edge of the track. The wide variety of molluscs in the rhynes include the nationally rare Pea Mussel.

Redwing

Buzzard

Common toad

Thrush

Adder with young

Badger

The main conservation problems in this section of the Walk is seeing that the rhynes are cleared sensitively. Rhynes become silted up and have to be dredged periodically. Local Inland Drainage Boards are responsible for this work which is increasingly done using heavy machinery. To ensure that the clearing is done with minimum of damage to the animal and plant life in the rhynes, Tony and Faith Moulin needed to make contact with the Drainage Boards, which was initially difficult as several different boards are involved in this small area.

Sandford and Winscombe

This section between the A368 at Sandford and the tunnel is very varied. In places the track is level with the surrounding land, while elsewhere it is on an embankment or in a cutting. There are also two diversions, where the trackbed was sold before the Walk came into existence, and an urban area through Winscombe village.

Alongside Sandford Station, where the path has been diverted from the original track, the absence of hardcore has permitted lush growth which perpetually threatens to close the path, with tall grasses, Nettles, Hogweed and Hemp Agrimony at the foot of a bramble-covered hedgerow.

In those cuttings where the banks have fairly recently been cleared of scrub, they are covered with Bramble, interwoven with climbers like Honeysuckle and Great Bindweed, while Hawthorn, Blackthorn and Dog Rose are beginning to emerge. Between the banks and the trackbed is a lush growth of tall grasses, nettles and Hogweed and, where these have been cleared, shorter grasses and woodland glade flowers such as Greater Stitchwort and Germander Speedwell.

In most of the cuttings the banks are covered with a scrub of Hawthorn, Blackthorn, Hazel and Elder, with saplings of mainly Ash and some Oak and Sycamore, the Bramble being partly suppressed by the shade. The ground flora is thin and patchy with Cleavers (*Galium aparine*), Common Toadflax, Herb Robert and Bush Vetch, depending on the degree of shade.

Where the Ash, Oak and Sycamores are large enough to give a canopy, the scrub itself is thinner, and the nettles and tall grasses have given way to woodland plants. These include Enchanter's Nightshade (*Circaea lutetiana*), Ivy, Cuckoo Pint, Hart's Tongue Fern and Dog' Mercury.

Where the verges are in sunlight, especially where the track is at or above the level of the surrounding land, stands of Rose-bay Willowherb and patches of Marjoram give variety.

The shunting yards at Sandford and the station area at Winscombe have typical station site vegetation with Buddleia, Cotoneasters, Rose-bay and Hairy Willowherb, Marjoram, Common Toadflax and Wild Carrot, all of which spread to the places where the track is above or level with the surrounding land. In connection with the Millennium Green development at Winscombe Station site, a local resident in July 1997 identified 30 species of flowering plants there, including 113 species of shrubs and trees. Similar detailed studies elsewhere on the line might also show great variety. Among the conspicuous flowers less common elsewhere on the line are a large patch of Pyrenean Cranesbill by the station platform at Winscombe, and on the nearby Woodborough Road bridge, masses of Valerian.

South of the bridge, residents bordering the line have influenced the flora by selective cutting back of vegetation and providing garden escapes, both from seeds travelling and from the dumping of garden waste. In the dry area near the bridge this gives a very varied flora with the station site vegetation supplemented by exotics and native plants uncommon in the area. Fennel grows in profusion and there is also the rare Red Orpine which attracts the Small Copper butterfly, the sweet smelling Winter Heliotrope and both White and Yellow Melilot.

On the west side this changes to a variable scrub of hedgerow plants, in which Blackthorn or Hawthorn may predominate with occasional larger trees. This continues, with a few interruptions, almost to the tunnel. On the east side is a patchwork alongside the gardens, then grassy banks with primroses and cowslips, alternating with Blackthorn scrub. Past the houses, where there is pasture below the level of the track, the hedges and the scrub support Narrow-leaved Everlasting Pea (*Lathyrus sylvestris*) as well as the more usual Bush Vetch and other climbers.

The mixed vegetation in the whole of this section supports a wide variety of insects through the Summer, and this combined with the Autumn supply of blackberries, spindle berries, hips, haws, hazel nuts and sloes attract all comers. The common woodland and garden birds can be seen or heard all the way from Sandford to the tunnel. In addition to those found all along the line are Woodpigeons, Collared Doves, Jays, Greater Spotted and Green Woodpeckers, Goldfinches, Blackcaps (all-year residents in this area) and, in summer, Willow and Garden warblers. House Sparrows and Starlings are noticeable in the built-up areas, where the woodland birds are less common.

Squirrels are numerous and Slowworms may be found in any part of this section.

The common butterflies – Brimstone, Small White, Small Tortoiseshell, Peacock and Comma, and later in the summer, Gatekeeper and Red Admiral – are found all along, but particularly in the more open areas such as the station sites where they are conspicuous on the Buddleias. Small numbers of Common and Holly Blue butterflies can also be seen in the more open areas, as well as the Marbled Whites which lay their eggs on grassland. These open area are also ideal for grasshoppers and Glowworms.

The Tunnel

The northern end of the tunnel is approached through a deep cutting with Goat Willow, Field Maple, Dogwood and Blackthorn at the entrance, then thick scrub with Ash, Field Maple, Hazel and some Sycamore, Hawthorn and Blackthorn. On the ground are woodland plants including Lesser Celandines, Wood

Violets, Cuckoo-pint, Ivy and Black Bryony.

This habitat is continuous with the woodland above the tunnel, providing the usual woodland birds, and mammals, while the shade also attracts the Speckled Wood butterfly.

The tunnel itself is different from anything else along the line, with no flowering plants in the dark central part. Towards the exits, there is increasing growth and variety of lichens, algae, liverworts, mosses, and then ferns, particularly the Hart's Tongue, and flowering plants tolerant of shade.

Bats are very occasionally reported in the tunnel, but, probably due to the cold winds, have never roosted. The only noticeable live invertebrates are small cave spiders. More readily seen are flies and bees which have become embedded in the 'stalactites'.

The banks of the deep and narrow cutting in hard limestone rock at the southern end of the tunnel have Ash, Hazel, Holm Oak (*Quercus ilex*), Field Maple and Holly, growing wherever there is sufficient soil, giving a heavy shade, so that only plants requiring little soil and light and liking the damp situation can flourish. Ferns include Maidenhair Spleenwort, Hart's Tongue, Male Fern and Polypody while a wide variety of woodland flowering plants including Wood Spurge, Ivy, Dog's Mercury and Bush Vetch cover the verges or decorate the rock faces along with the ferns, mosses and liverworts.

As the cutting widens out, a variety of flowering plants suited to partial shade, such as Yellow Archangel and Nettle-leaved Bellflower grow happily on the verges, while Herb Robert, Wild Strawberry, and the occasional Common Spotted Orchid emerge from cracks in the rock wall between the trailing Ivy. As the cutting widens further, the trees include Elder, Dogwood, Hawthorn and Oak, and the varied woodland ground flora is gradually replaced by Brambles and Nettles.

The woodland here joins that above and around the tunnel, and so has the same types of woodland birds, mammals and butterflies, with the addition of rabbits coming in sometimes from the more open ground beyond.

The Southern Slope

Beyond the cutting south of the tunnel, the track is on a high embankment on a south-facing limestone hillside with only a thin covering of soil. Several groups of mature trees, mainly Sycamore, Ash and Beech, are established on the embankment on the west side. The banks also have large areas of scrub, which may be predominantly Blackthorn, Hazel or Hawthorn mixed with Bramble and containing Field Maple and a group of Spindle Trees. Where the scrub cover has been cleared from the verges or banks there is species-rich limestone grassland where, in addition to the usual Common Ragwort, Bird's-foot Trefoil and Marjoram you can find Ploughman's Spikenard, Hairy St John's Wort, Wild Basil, Basil-Thyme, and the drought resistant Silver Ragwort (*Senecio cineraria*). Common Mullein and the occasional Dark Mullein grow in the open ground on the west side of the embankment facing Kings Wood and in the stretch between the A38 and the Axbridge by-pass. Narrow-leaved Everlasting Pea is noticeable on the fences and the edges of higher vegetation.

Rabbits find conditions ideal. Numbers rise to a peak, making conditions ideal for the spread of disease, so numbers crash. During the population explosions they can be seen on the track and in surrounding fields all the way from the tunnel cutting to the Axbridge By-pass lay-by.

Buzzards are often seen circling overhead, on the lookout for Rabbits or small rodents when the weather is suitable. Otherwise the birds seen here are those found along the whole length of the line.

Adders may be spotted in the morning sun, warming themselves to a working level.

The flowers here particularly attract a variety of blue and brown butterflies, especially the Common Blue, the Gatekeeper and the Small-Copper. The day-flying Cinnabar Moth is found while its tiger-striped caterpillars are readily seen eating the leaves of Ragwort. Like the frequently seen shiny black Bloody-nosed Beetle (*Timarcha tenebricosa*), they rely on warning colours rather than concealment.

The Axbridge-Cheddar Cycleway

The Cycleway came into existence more recently than the rest of the Walk, and a larger proportion of it is not on the original trackbed, so the flora, and in consequence the fauna, will take time to settle down. Any account of it will therefore need to be revised sooner than some other parts of the Walk.

The most recent survey was carried out in November 1995 by the Moss Group of the Somerset Wildlife Trust West Mendip Survey Team. In addition to their detailed study of mosses, they made a brief general report on the natural history of this section. As elsewhere on the line, the variations in vegetation across the track are much greater than those along it, with the zones along the edge of the track being generally similar to the corresponding zones along the rest of the Walk.

The track itself, which is free of vegetation, is edged by a narrow band of Annual Meadowgrass, mixed with Biting Stonecrop, Ribwort Plantain, Lesser Trefoil and Ox-eye Daisy. This grades into a wider zone of short, species-rich grassland containing Wild Carrot, Lambs Lettuce, Cut-leaved Cranesbill, Bush Vetch, Common Toadflax, Annual Meadowgrass, Creeping Cinquefoil and Sticky Mouse-ear. Further out is long coarse grassland dominated by Cocksfoot, with Common Bent, Nettle, Hogweed, White Deadnettle and some False Brome and Field Horsetail. This may reach to the fence, but along most of the length, the Cycleway land is wide enough to include a further habitat.

Beyond the verges there are four main habitats. First, there is a wide band of open rough grassland from the By-pass almost up to Holwell Lane, and then a short distance of partly improved grassland. Beyond this, up to Fiveways Bridge, is scrub and woodland in what was a railway cutting. Finally, there is a narrow corridor between new housing and an industrial estate.

The higher ground near the by-pass has mainly disturbed-ground species such as Rough, and Smooth Hawksbeard. In the Spring there are Horsetail and Coltsfoot, followed in the

Summer by Ox-eye Daisy, Marjoram, Tufted Vetch, Wild Carrot, Catsear, Black Medick, Agrimony, White, and Red Clover, Fleabane and the rare Thyme-leaved Sandwort, with Common Toadflax in the Autumn. In the wetter areas at the bottom of the slope are Common Reed and Wood Small-Reed (*Calamagrostis epigejos*). A selection of native trees have been planted along this stretch of grassland, and some bluebells and cultivated daffodils at the picnic site.

In the improved grassland near Holwell Lane, alongside the Wild Carrot we have Yarrow, Meadow Peaflower, occasional Clustered Bellflower and later, Common Toadflax and Purple Loosestrife.

The wooded cutting towards Fiveways Bridge has high banks with overhanging trees, patches of thick scrub and a drainage ditch. The banks of the cutting are covered with Bramble, Old Mans Beard, Ivy, White bryony and Great Bindweed. Hemp Agrimony and Rose-bay Willowherb are dominant at the base, with Greater Burnet Saxifrage, Hogweed and Hedge Woundwort in the damp areas. In the ditch itself, Hemlock Water Dropwort is conspicuous in the Summer, and among the rarities are Water Betony and Brooklime. The main shrubs, as elsewhere, are Hawthorn, Blackthorn and Dogwood and, as in the damper sections elsewhere, willows.

The gravelled area near Fiveways Bridge, the site of the loading platform, has station site flora including Small Toadflax, Rue-leaved Saxifrage, Common Whitlow Grass and Procumbent Pearlwort. The narrow stretch between Fiveways Bridge and the end of the Cycleway has plants typical of an urban building site.

The birds found commonly on the rest of the Walk are also to be seen on the Cycleway. The recently disturbed ground near the by-pass also attracts Goldfinches, while the reservoir is a haunt of a wide variety of wildfowl, many of which fly over the path in daily or annual migrations. The wooded region in the cutting is an excellent nesting area for small birds.

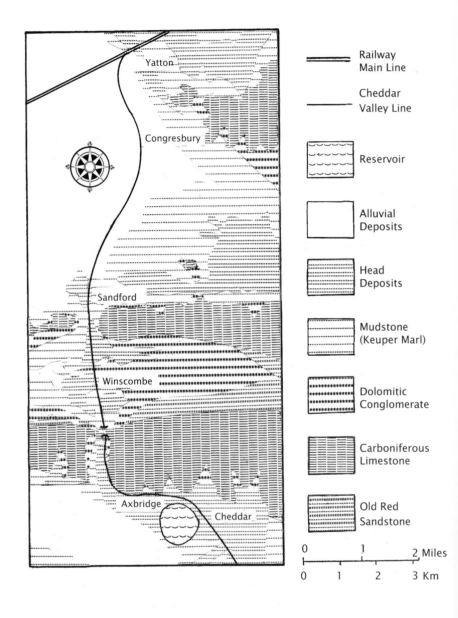

Railway
Main Line

Cheddar
Valley Line

Reservoir

Alluvial
Deposits

Head
Deposits

Mudstone
(Keuper Marl)

Dolomitic
Conglomerate

Carboniferous
Limestone

Old Red
Sandstone

Yatton

Congresbury

Sandford

Winscombe

Axbridge

Cheddar

0   1   2 Miles

0   1   2   3 Km

5 GEOLOGY OF THE ROUTE

General Geology

In addition to studies on particular aspects of the geology of the Mendip Hills area, several general accounts have been published, recent ones being those of Alabaster (1982), Simms (1997) and Farrant & Smart (1997). We will give a simplified description of those features relevant to the route of the Cheddar Valley Line.

The northern end of the route starts in the North Somerset Levels, which cover most of the area between Bristol and the Mendip Hills. The southern end, including the continuation to Wells and beyond, runs along the borderline between the Mendips and the main Somerset Levels which cover much of the land between the Mendip Hills and the Quantocks. The central part of the route goes through the Mendip Hills themselves. The three main types of land - the hills, the margins of the hills, and the levels, each have a characteristic geology, affecting their form, land use, flora and fauna, and consequently their whole appearance.

The Mendip Hills

The Mendip Hills largely determine the geology of the whole route of the Cheddar Valley Railway from Yatton to Wells, and beyond along the East Somerset Railway. While only part of the line is through the hills, the rest is affected by the streams running down the hillsides, and the debris they have washed down. While the lower surrounding land has been shaped by events which, geologically speaking, are recent, the composition and shape of the hills themselves result from a long and varied history. The underlying continental plate is believed to have been moving progressively northwards,

61

starting from latitudes well south of the Equator more than 400 million years ago, and passing through a succession of climatic zones while rocks were formed, eroded or modified.

Today the Mendips consist of a core of Devonian Old Red Sandstone 380-360 million years old, overlain by layers of Carboniferous Limestone deposited during successive immersions in warm shallow seas 360-300 million years ago. In the Western Mendips much of the limestone has been eroded, mainly by rain, frost and wind, so that on some of the hilltops, the surface rock is sandstone. This gives a localised acid and sometimes waterlogged soil, where heather and other acid-loving plants contrast with the vegetation of the well-drained limestone on the rest of the hillsides. The largest such area is Blackdown, the highest point on Mendip, but the sandstone also outcrops close to the railway track at Church Knoll in Winscombe, just west of the tunnel, and at Hale, a little to the east of it. The carboniferous limestone layers can be seen in exposed cliffs and excavations along the south-west side of the hills and, on our route, in the railway tunnel and at the western end of the Axbridge by-pass.

During the Triassic age (c. 250 million years ago), the hills were exposed to a hot arid climate with spasmodic very heavy rainfall, when gravel, stones and even large rocks loosened, by erosion, were washed down into the valley. Later in the same era these accumulated screes of grey limestone and red sandstone were embedded in fresh limestone and marl, giving the attractive-looking Dolomitic Conglomerate found widely around Mendip and used to build the stations and bridges of the Cheddar Valley Railway. It contains stones of different colours, which may be large, small, rounded or angular, and numerous or thinly scattered, embedded in a limestone matrix which is usually reddish but occasionally is buff coloured. House or garden walls may be seen throughout the area where adjacent stones, until they are weathered, have strikingly different appearances.

This Conglomerate occurs in the valleys and particularly

Top: Dolomitic Conglomerate.

Bottom: Potato Stones cut and uncut.

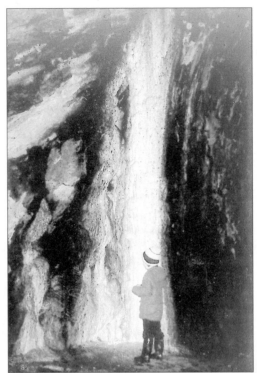

Left: The stalactite column at the junction of the lined and bare rock parts of the tunnel.

Below: Tunnel, north entrance.

at the exits to the valleys all round the Mendips. As these weathering conditions have recurred, the deposition of screes has been repeated, often in the same places, in later periods. While limestone is hard, it can be dissolved chemically by acidic rainwater, which forms cracks, crevices, channels and ultimately caves. Some time after these rocks were formed, water coming from below as warm springs, deposited various minerals, including metallic sulphides, in crevices and pockets in the limestone. Some of these, such as Galena (lead sulphide) remained mainly in the form in which they were deposited, while the sulphides of zinc, cadmium and iron were more often converted to carbonates or oxides. Apart from lead, only Calamine (zinc carbonate) has been of serious commercial importance, though Pyrolusite (manganese dioxide) and Celestine (strontium sulphate) were mined in a small way, and a number of small Ochre mines (iron oxide for use as a pigment) were worked successfully, mainly in the twentieth century.

Because the limestone was laid down in separate layers over a long period of time, and has had an even longer subsequent history, there are many local differences within the general pattern. The lower layers immediately above the Old Red Sandstone are interlaced with layers of shale, which contains clay, and so are less permeable to water. The rainwater from above now seeps freely through the upper limestone until it reaches the water table of the layers below. Along the south-western face of Mendip, porous limestone continues laterally under the relatively impermeable clay at the foot of the hills, so the water emerges at the lowest limestone outcrop as a spring or 'rising'. The consequent line of risings where it emerges round the edge of Mendip provides the location of villages in the area, notably along the old railway route from Axbridge to Wells.

The Margins of the Hills

The Mendip Hills have a steep slope along the entire south-western face, giving quite a narrow band of eroded debris on this side. On the north-eastern side, and in wider valleys like the Vale of Winscombe, where the slope is shallower and longer, more debris has been spread over a larger area. It has in consequence been sorted to a much greater extent, so that broken limestone and sandstone change only gradually to the more completely weathered marls.

Among the deposits in the fringes of Mendip are the decorative 'potato stones'. These are vaguely rounded silica nodules, typically about 3 inches in diameter, with concentric coloured layers, mostly pink and white and, in the centre, a space surrounded by quartz crystals or sometimes calcite. These have been formed by gradual replacement by silica of anhydrite (calcium sulphate), where it occurs in inclusions during seepage of silica-rich water. These stones are found particularly on Sandford Hill, and in the spoil workings south of the tunnel.

Keuper Marl, a limy mudstone, coloured dark red with iron oxide, derived from wind-blown Triassic dust and silt, which is very evident in the railway cutting north of the tunnel, is found where the margins of the hills spread out to the levels.

Some glacial deposits have been found in the coastal part of North Somerset, Devon and Cornwall, but nowhere else south of the Severn. This is therefore regarded as the southern limit of glaciation in the west of England. Just beyond the actual glacial area, there are periglacial or 'head' deposits where soil or scree have been moved progressively downhill by repeated freezing and thawing, giving an earthy mass with angular fragments. Head deposits provide the surface soil in parts of the Vale of Winscombe and valleys bordering the Mendips

The Levels

The levels both north and south of the Mendips have a covering of deposits from slow-flowing rivers and streams, bringing fine debris from weathered rocks in the Mendips and elsewhere. This has been moved around and supplemented by periodic flooding by fresh or salt water, giving deposits of alluvial mud and silty sands.

Much of the land between the Mendips and the Quantocks was near or below mean sea level within the last few thousand years, when the alluvial deposits from the rivers and the sea became covered by layers of peat which are much thicker and more extensive than those in the north. Beween the Mendips and Bristol, the hills merge more gradually into the levels, giving a different and more complicated picture, with more blue alluvial clay and silty sands on the surface.

The Route

From Yatton, where the Branch Railway left the main east-west line, through Congresbury and almost to Sandford, the land is flat and almost at sea level. The soil is generally a grey silty clay deposited by marine flooding in Romano-British times or earlier. A large pottery kiln existed at Congresbury, while grey Roman sherds are often found near the line.

Because the land is flat and low-lying, the fields are divided by drainage ditches and, except during a drought, there is a high water table. While wheat has been an important crop in the past, the land is now used mainly for pasture, particularly dairy farming. For the first few decades of the Cheddar Valley branch line, a milk processing factory operated at Yatton, bottling milk and making milk products.

Approaching Sandford, the line goes over Ice Age Head Deposits of stony debris of limestone and cherts which produced soils which drain poorly.The line passes within yards of the western end of Sandford Hill, where limestone was quarried until 1970. For very many years the stone was loaded in the quarry on to trucks which were then shunted on to a private siding by Sandford Station for rail haulage elsewhere. There were small quarries and mines for Galena, Calamine and Ochre at many points on the hill.

Just south of Sandford Hill is a belt of poorly-drained land with grey subsoil where Towerhead Brook goes under the line, but in most of the Vale of Winscombe, between Sandford Hill and Winscombe Hill, the soil derives from a chocolate coloured Keuper Marl, with occasional local outcrops of Triassic Conglomerate. The very recognisable stone in these outcrops consists of Dolomitic Conglomerate containing broken fragments of older limestone, sandstone and other debris. Layers of this conglomerate have been exposed in the building of several roads in the village of Winscombe, and are seen between the pavement and the front garden fences, and the soil near these outcrops contains a lot of debris from the weathered stone. There are also remains of a small lead or zinc mine in a garden in The Green, a road in the centre of Winscombe village.

The Vale of Winscombe supported predominantly mixed farming.

The northern side of Winscombe Hill is made of Keuper Marl, so both the tunnel approach and the northern part of the tunnel itself were cut through this material. It is soft, so the engineers had to line this part of the tunnel, which they did with the bricks and the blocks of Dolomitic Conglomerate seen today. A wall of the same stone was built in the tunnel approach to prevent soil falling into the cutting, and still does its job, but elsewhere in the cutting, landslip is a problem after heavy rain, when the Keuper Marl becomes saturated.

Just over half-way through the tunnel there is a change to hard limestone, where lining of the tunnel was not needed and the rock strata are clearly visible, both in the tunnel and in the rocky cutting to the south. Water drips from the roof, and runs down the walls throughout the tunnel, but much more in the lined part of the tunnel, where the earth above is Keuper Marl, than in the unlined part, where it is limestone, and is greatest at the junction of the two. The water comes down as rain, is acidified by the carbon dioxide in the atmosphere and the soil, and on its passage through the rock (or the mortar) dissolves some of the limestone. Emerging drop by drop into the tunnel, it loses a little of the carbon dioxide, becomes less acid and consequently deposits some of the limestone. In enclosed caves this process leads to the slow formation of stalactites and stalagmites. In the tunnel, where ventilation is much greater, the loss of carbon dioxide is faster and there is also evaporation of water, so limestone is deposited more rapidly. This gives a softer limestone deposit known as 'tufa', which appears on the roof as thin limestone tubes or 'straw stalactites' which break off as soon as their weight is too much for their frail stems. These straw stalactites can also be seen under the bridges between Sandford and the tunnel.

Where the water flow is greatest, at the junction of the lined and unlined parts of the tunnel, a stalactite-like column has formed on the western side. Here the deposit is harder, forming a glossy white surface with dark spots which are the remains of insects embedded in the deposited limestone.

In the wider and higher unlined part of the tunnel south of the 'stalactite' column, the different strata of rock can be seen running obliquely along the walls and across the roof, dipping towards the southern exit at 20 to 30 degrees. Thick limestone layers are interspersed with thinner layers of shale, containing cherts. The strata may have alternate pink and greenish tints due to different minerals, which also colour the limestone deposits which have been formed since the tunnel was built.

South of the tunnel, until the line descends between Axbridge and Cheddar, the route is on limestone with a thin covering of soil, and the land is used mainly for pasture, especially sheep. The underlying strata can be seen very well along the side of the by-pass opposite Axbridge Station buildings. As elsewhere, local mineral inclusions have been found, particularly Yellow Ochre on Axbridge Hill. This was extracted for use in paints, mainly in the 20th Century, especially in the 1930s when it was transported down the hill in trucks. The capstan and the remains of the narrow gauge rails are still in the ground just above Axbridge. Manganese ores were also once worked on Shute Shelve.

Axbridge and Cheddar are two of the string of villages along the bottom of the escarpment edge where the water, passing through the caves and the permeable limestone, emerges at the lowest limestone outcrop. Where the route leaves the limestone to go down to Cheddar, the soil is mainly the same Head as near Sandford, except where soil has been moved in railway or cycleway construction.

The marl on the lower south-facing slopes is quite fertile, and the warm position, the good drainage and the good water supply has made the area very suitable for growing strawberries and other market garden crops, which provided much of the trade of the Cheddar Valley Railway.

6 The Walks

Footpaths meet or cross the Railway Walk all the way from Yatton to Cheddar, so you can go for quite a variety of walks which include different stretches of the railway track and finish at your starting point. We offer here a selection of such walks. As some cross or overlap one another, it is easy to make permutations or combinations of them which are longer, shorter, or just different.

If there are climbs or particularly wet or muddy areas, we have mentioned this at the beginning of each walk. The climbs rarely involve a rise of more than 50 ft., and only in one or two walks does the overall climb exceed 100 ft. While in anything but exceptional weather, ordinary good walking shoes are usually appropriate, the footpaths in the levels are often very wet. Naturally, walkers must use their common sense about the possibility of replacement of stiles by gates, gates by stiles, or other local changes.

Although the directions we have given should suffice, a walking map (1:25,000) is an asset. Ordnance Survey Explorer 154 (Bristol West & Portishead) covers walks 2 & 3 from Yatton and the one from Congresbury. Those from all other starting points are covered by Explorer 141 (Cheddar Gorge & Mendip Hills West), except for a few yards in Barton on Winscombe Walk 4 which are on Explorer 153 (Weston-super-Mare & Bleadon Hill). The entire length of the Railway Walk (Yatton walk 1), is covered by Explorers 154 plus 141.

For walks going through the tunnel, even though the light inside during daylight hours is usually sufficient, it is worth while taking a torch to look closely at the stalactites and other features on the walls. For those who would prefer not to go through the tunnel on these routes, we have included an alternative permissive footpath which goes above the tunnel instead of through it. This is given in the appropriate Winscombe Walks.

The buses given are First Bus/Badgerline, and only include routes which currently run throughout the day. We have not included times or frequencies which, in any case, are subject to change.

We have indicated the location of refreshment places near the starting (and finishing) points in the various villages and elsewhere as appropriate.

While we have made every effort to ensure that the paths indicated are open to the public, the fact that they are given here cannot be regarded as evidence that they are rights-of way. We are not aware of any problems of access on the routes described here. Walkers should, of course, respect the country code, close gates after them, keep dogs under strict control, and leave no litter.

WALK FROM YATTON

The starting point for the Yatton walks is the entrance to the Railway Walk on the south side of Yatton Station (GR42 5661).

On Foot: From the centre of Yatton go north along High Street, then left just before the railway bridge, with the station on your right and through the car park to the end, where the entry to the Railway Walk will be signposted.
By Train: Bristol - Weston-super-Mare - Taunton local trains stop here. Leave from the down (south) side and turn right.
By Bus: Bristol - Clevedon (355/360) and Weston-super-Mare - Clevedon (823). Get out at Station Road, go over the road bridge and turn right.
Refreshments: The Railway Inn at the station, other inns in High Street and a cafe in the shopping precinct.

Yatton - Cheddar Linear Walk

10 Miles, almost entirely railway gradients.

Can be muddy in places where the path has been diverted from the trackbed. Otherwise a good walking surface. For anyone walking the entire route starting from Yatton or Cheddar, there is no convenient way back by public transport. However, starting from Weston-super-Mare it is possible to take an early train to Yatton station (c12 minutes), walk to Winscombe (6 miles), Axbridge (8.5) or Cheddar (10) and return to Weston on a 126 bus (50 minutes from Cheddar).

The first quarter of a mile of the route was for a long time a derelict stretch of the station site and only recently became part of the Railway Walk. It is bordered by dense blackthorn scrub where a variety of small birds nest in Spring and a range of butterflies can be seen throughout the Summer. In Winter, with the wide assortment of berries, this is one of the largest local feeding grounds for mixed flocks of thrushes, including resident blackbirds, song and mistle thrushes and the migrant redwings and fieldfares.

Beyond this, where the route has been managed as a walk and nature reserve for years, there are wide grassy borders and rhynes on both sides with hedges between the rhynes and the pasture of the flat surrounding land. At intervals along the route all the way to Sandford are culverts for water to drain from east to west under the track. These were constructed when the railway was built, and the original battlement topped brickwork is still there, rarely needing repair except where it has been damaged by modern drainage equipment.

About half a mile along the track is a large pond behind the hedge on the left. This was created during the construction of the railway, is part of the drainage system and has a path round both sides. Moorhens, toads and occasionally swans breed there. By the pond is a footpath giving access to Yatton village, which can be seen on the left with its truncated spire. Straight ahead in the distance is Congresbury, where the church has a long pointed spire.

After a further half mile you have to cross a wooden footbridge over the rhyne on the right to reach Moor Lane, as the old railway bridge over the River Yeo was demolished when the railway closed. Go left along Moor Lane which takes you over the Yeo to the A370, where you go left along the pedestrian path, passing railwaymens' cottages on the opposite side. Cross the road at the traffic island, and re-enter the Railway Walk next to the bus stop lay-by. You are now on the site of Congresbury Station, which was the junction for the Wrington Vale Light Railway.

On the left is the former stationmaster's house and in the centre the remains of the platform. The main track continues straight ahead, while the track of the Wrington Vale Line diverges very slightly to the left and then disappears into private land. On the right is a pond connected with a very extensive reed bed, which is a breeding ground for reed and sedge warblers and reed buntings. Beyond this, the track is crossed by a lane with access to Congresbury village.

For nearly two miles the line is bordered by level pasture on both sides, except for a golf course half-way along, and then comes a major diversion where land had been sold to local farmers soon after the railway closed. John Thatcher, the owner of one of these farms, has allowed a permissive path through his land, which is now waymarked.

There is a fence across the entire track with a stile on to a drove with a second stile opposite carrying a notice about a a cutting. The noticeable features along here are a flight of steps up on both sides installed by the railway to give a footway crossing and, a little later, two typical Bristol & Exeter stone bridges over the track. The first bridge carries a farm crossing

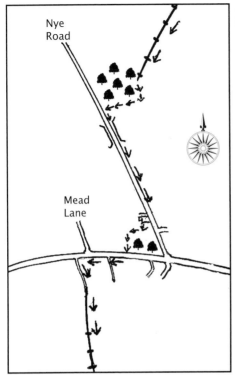

Nye
Road

Mead
Lane

permissive path. Cross both stiles and go down a flight of steps on the right into an orchard. Turn left and follow the path round two sides of the orchard, emerging on to a minor road, Nye Road, where you turn left over the old railway bridge which crosses the former track, now levelled.

Half a mile along Nye Road are footpath signs both left and right. Take the one to the right for a few yards along a tarmac entry to an industrial site. A second sign on the left takes you across a yard to a signed permissive path into an orchard. Here you go right, following the path round two sides of the orchard to a stile on to Station Road, Sandford. Cross the road and go right, passing 'The Railway Inn'; opposite, with an original railway signal and where refreshment is available.

Nearly a quarter of a mile along is Sandford Station, a listed building which is well kept, largely intact and worth a visit. It is now the premises of the Sandford Stone Centre, which sells garden ornaments and paving (and has a cafe). A few yards to the right of Sandford Stone is Cothill Lane, and 150 yards along the lane on the left is a waymarked stile on to the diverted Railway Walk. The path is very narrow to start with, but widens and then leads on to the old railway track and sidings.

The track continues through scrub and woodland, at first at or slightly above the surrounding land, and then goes into, and the second, an unclassified road to the cemetery.

Immediately after the second bridge, the path goes up a ramp on the right to leave the cutting which has been taken over by garden extensions. You are now in Winscombe, where most of the village is on your left, while the land on the right, at the present time, is mostly pasture. The path soon rejoins the original track, going over an accommodation bridge on to Winscombe Station site, now being partly restored as the village Millennium Green.

The track leaves the station site, crossing the Woodborough Road bridge whose history has been recounted in Chapter 3. It continues through the village, under a road bridge built by the railway, past the recreation ground, and emerges between fields used for pasture. Winscombe Parish Church, in the old village of Winscombe, can be seen up on the hillside on the right.

The track now goes into a heavily wooded cutting and through the tunnel under the Mendips, which has been described in Chapters 3 and 5. The walls of the cutting beyond the tunnel are initially very high, but the track soon emerges from between these fern and moss covered cliffs to take you along an embankment and over an accommodation bridge above pasture land with views across to wooded hills on both sides. The village of Cross is seen ahead, with the levels beyond it stretching into the distance.

The track goes down to the A38 where, in place of the bridge demolished long ago, there is a traffic island and metal barriers to guide you across. The path climbs up again on to the old track where the land rises on the left to Shute Shelve and falls away on the right to the levels, giving panoramic views.

About one third of a mile after the A38, the railway track has been taken over by the Axbridge by-pass, with the path ending in a lay-by with an information signboard, car park and picnic site. Going through Axbridge is now a pleasant necessity. Take the slip road down on the right immediately before the lay-by. It is one-way for motor traffic to come up, with a 'down' cycleway on the left. At the bottom of this road is a multiple junction (see map). Follow the footpath round to the left behind the barriers and then across two roads. Passing Houlgate Way (on your right), enter the now fairly quiet road lined on both sides by houses which are clearly part of the old town. This is West Street which leads into High Street and finally the Square.

There are interesting old buildings all round, Axbridge having been an administrative centre since Saxon times. The most striking building, where High Street enters the Square is called 'King John's Hunting Lodge'. King John did hunt in this area, but the building is actually a late Mediaeval merchants house. Up on the left at the opposite end of the Square is St. John's church dating from the early 1400s.

A short diversion here up the footpath to the left of the church, then up the steps to the right just after the churchyard, will take you to the old station. You can then come down through the other side of the churchyard, back to the Square.

Around the Square are several refreshment places, and facing the church at the same end is the Town Hall. Leaving the Square past the Town Hall you enter Cheddar Road, which will take you to the by-pass where, a few yards along, opposite the drive of St. Michael's Cheshire Homes, is the entrance to the Axbridge-Cheddar Cycleway.

The Cycleway is partly but not entirely along the old railway track. It first descends to pass close to the reservoir constructed in the 1930s, which, apart from storing water, is a sailing and fishing amenity and a breeding, feeding and resting site for a variety of wildfowl. There is a picnic site here with good views in several directions. The track continues through a wooded cutting and under Fiveways Bridge, a typical Bristol & Exeter construction. For the final one third of a mile the route is guided between housing and industrial estates to Station Road. Before reaching Station Road it passes the old station site where surviving parts of the old station can be seen between other industrial premises and the stone which the present occupants of the site use for their work of church restoration.

At Station Road, a left turn and a walk of a third of a mile along Station Road and Bath Road will take you to the Market Cross which has a bus stop (126, Wells - Weston-super-Mare) and is in the centre of the village and the shopping area.

YATTON - WALK 2

Yatton Pond - Cadbury Farm - Cadbury Hill - Claverham - Stowey Road

5 Miles, one moderate climb.

From the Railway Station, follow the trackbed of the Railway Walk, crossing the stiles and barriers. After about half a mile you pass a large pond seen through the hedge on the left. After another quarter of a mile pass the second of two large ash trees on your left and, at the next farm crossing, turn left into a field which has public access and follow the track up through the field to Cadbury Farm.

Turn right into Cadbury Farm Road, a modern housing development, and right again into Mendip Road. Pass the playing field on your left and the sheltered housing 'Housing 21' on your right. When you reach the main road (B3133), turn left along it and cross when it is safe to do so. With a large cedar tree in front of you, turn left into Henley Lane, past Claverham Cricket Club and its car park and continue up this lane until you see another car park on your right with an information board. Walk through the car park on to the continuation of your track, turning right almost immediately

Cross the road by the old Methodist Chapel, now a private house, pass the Post Office, then turn left into Chestnut Drive.

At the end of Chestnut Drive turn left, then after 50 yards turn right where you see a Public Footpath sign. Go down the lane and through Streamcross Farm, through several fields following waymarks, back to Yatton.

As you reach the houses, fork right past the gardens to come out by Hangstones playing field in Stowey Road, a 1960s housing development. Go right along Stowey Road until you reach the fifth turning left, Barberry Farm Road. Turn left into Barberry Farm Road and notice the fine old farmhouse on the left which has been modernised. At the junction with Yatton High Street turn right, and after about 150 yards you will return to the station.

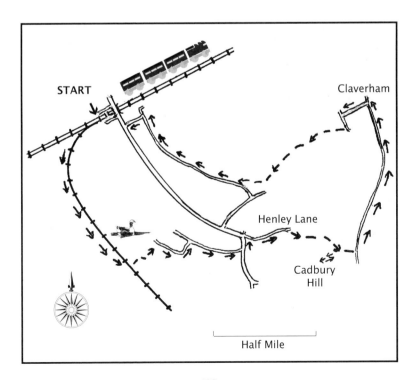

YATTON WALK 3

Gang Wall - Wemberham Lane - The Grange - Middle Rhyne - Biddle Street

6.5 Miles, level ground, may be wet in places. An optional short cut leaving out The Grange and Middle Rhyne gives a walk of 3.5 miles.

From the station follow the Cheddar Valley Railway path for about half a mile until you see a large pond through the hedge on your left, followed immediately by a 'footpath crossroads' at a point where you can clearly see Yatton village on the left. Turn right, crossing two stiles and you are walking on a raised linear wooded path, Gangwall, which is an ancient causeway and sea defence.

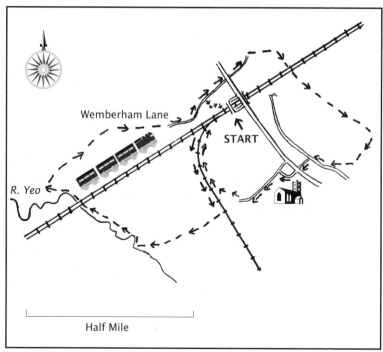

When you reach the river Yeo, do not cross the footbridge but, keeping the river Yeo on your left, turn right along the often wet and muddy footpath which is roughly parallel to the top of the near riverbank. On your left you pass Pilhay Farm, a modern farmhouse built on the site of a very old dwelling. Keeping straight on you will reach a well signed crossing point of the main line railway. Before crossing, take extra care to listen and look for trains, which approach very fast.

Continuing on a raised path, with the Yeo still on your left, brings you to another gate where you turn right through a stock pen leading to a house and a lane. Walk down this lane (Wemberham Lane) until, after about a mile, you cross an old railway bridge, from the former Yatton-Clevedon Line. On your left is a large privately-owned pond, stocked with fish, which was once a railway borrow-pit. Turn right among the new housing into Horsecastle Close. You will pass some old cottages and the old Evangelical Chapel, now a private house.

To shorten the walk, turn right past the Chapel into Wemberham Crescent. Walk straight ahead to a small path between the houses, leading to the station.

Cross Yatton High Street into the remnant of Moor Road. Passing the Grange on your left, you will meet the new road and turn left to come into Kenn Moor Road. After about 100 yards go over a stile on the right next to an iron gate (yellow arrow). Walk parallel to the hedge on the right as far as the rhyne, turn left and keep by the rhyne to a bridge, then diagonally right to a gate in the far right-hand corner. Keep on beside the rhyne to the main line railway crossing. Cross carefully to the footpath which follows an old trackway between fields and rhynes which have interesting wetland wildlife. Carry on for about one and a half miles, crossing over farm tracks until you are quite close to Streamcross Farm on your left, then cross the fields diagonally to your right towards Yatton. This will bring you into Stowey Road, a 1960s housing development, near Hangstones, the metal footbridge with a barbed wire fence on your left.

Turn right and pass Beech Road on your left, taking the next left hand turning at Well Lane, with the church in front of you. Cross the High Street and continue up Church Road. You could look in at the 'Cathedral of the Moors' as it was known and have a look at the 14th century Prebendal House by the church gate, the old school on your right, and Church House, once the church alehouse, but more recently the almshouse, now renovated by a housing association.

At the end of Church Road, turn left into Chescombe Road and walk along it until it peters out into a farm track which takes you past Rectory Farm on your right and a large pond on your left. The pond is the result of work during the construction of the Cheddar Valley Railway and formed part of the drainage system. It now has a dipping pond for wildlife studies and was the Wildlife and Wetlands Pond of the Year in 1991.

Continuing along the farm track, you turn right into the Railway Walk, and in about half a mile, are back at Yatton Station.

Walk from Congresbury

Dolemoor - Puxton - Pool Farm - Gang Wall - Yatton
Pond - Congresbury Church

7miles on level ground, partly in damp meadows

Starting Point: Car ark by Congresbury Millennium Green,
behind the bus stop by the river bridge on the A370.
(GR438639).

Buses: Bristol - Weston-super-Mare (350, 351,352,353);
Clevedon - Weston-super-Mare (823).

Refreshments: There are inns and cafes near the War
Memorial in the centre of the village

Walk beside the River Yeo through the Green and fields as far
as the bridge by the weir. Cross two footbridges and follow
the path before turning right by Weir Cottage. Pass the Bowling
Club on your left and keep to the right along Mill Leg, and
turn left at the end towards 'The Plough'. Cross over the B3133
(a busy road), turning left, then right at The Causeway.
Continue to the end of The Causeway, bearing left along the
drove, straight on at the junction past the fooball pitch on
your right until you turn into a small car park.

Follow the waymarked path, then go left over the bridge
and right along the rhyne. Cross three gates and the Railway
Walk, followed by a fourth gate. Continue straight on across a
metal footbridge with a barbed wire fence on your left.

Cross a stile and a plank bridge and immediately turn right.
Go through a gate and turn left into a lane, where there are
wooden chicken houses on the left. Go through a gate with a
bridge on the left, and immediately turn right, then go through
a gate and along a track. Turn left at a crossing track (Dolemoor

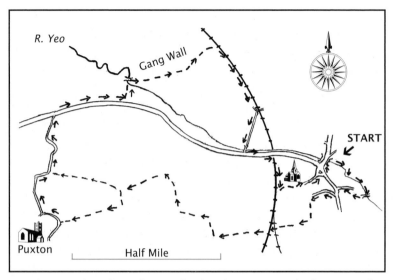

Lane) immediately in front of a derelict cottage and pass under an electric transmission line to stone bridges over the Meer Wall Rhyne and the Oldbridge River. The area between the stone bridges and Puxton is now a nature reserve owned and managed by the Wildlife Trust, while rhynes and the land bordering them have SSSI status.

A short cut saving half a mile may be taken by turning right down Goosey Drive (to the left of Oldbridge River), rejoining the walk by turning nght at Puxton Lane. However, Puxton Church is well worth a visit if you can spare the time.

Take the track ahead to the right of a ruin and in 250 yards follow the main track to the right, then turn right at the minor road in Puxton. Taking the next road left will enable you to visit the 13th Century Puxton Church with a leaning tower. After visiting the church, return to the point where you took this left turn and continue along Puxton Lane to the A370.

Cross and go right along the pedestrian path of the A370 for about half a mile until just after the small works on the left oppos;te the entrance to Moorham Park. Turn left across a field along a footpath signposted 'Yatton'. Cross the River Yeo at Pilhay Bridge and after 20 yards go over a waymarked stile. Follow the track with the rhyne on your right (Gang Wall) for about two thirds of a mile going over two stiles until you reach the Railway Walk.

Go right along the railway track and after a little over half a mile cross the wooden footbridge on the right to Moor Lane. Go left along Moor Lane and cross the Yeo to the A370, where you go left along the pedestrian path to the traffic island, where you cross the road and re-enter the Railway Walk next to the bus stop lay-by. You are now on the site of Congresbury Station, which was the junction for the Wrington Vale Light Railway. With the road behind you, the main track to Cheddar goes south with a line of boulders after about a quarter of a mile.

After the boulders, take a track to the left (Littlewall Drove) beside the rhyne (it is just past this point that the Wrington Vale Line branches off to the left from the main Cheddar Valley Line). Continue, with the rhyne on your left and the school across the field. Go over a waymarked stile and bridge, across the field and into the churchyard. Turn right before the church and out of the churchyard into Pauls Causeway. Turn left into Broad street, past the shops with Congresbury Cross at the end. Cross at the pedestrian lights, go over the bridge and back to the start.

Rhynes near Congresbury.

WALKS FROM WINSCOMBE

The starting point for the Winscombe walks is the site of Winscombe Station (GR418577), which becomes the Village Green on January 1st, 2000.

Bus: 126 (Weston-super-Mare - Wells). Get out at Browns Corner. From the side of the road opposite the bus shelter and the Woodborough, go to the corner and turn right down Woodborough Road almost to the railway bridge and go through the entrance on the right.

Refreshments: Varied refreshments are available at the Woodborough (150 yards into the shopping area from the bridge) and several premises opposite.

WINSCOMBE: CIRCULAR WALK 1

Nut Tree Farm - Max Mills - Rhodyate Farm - Ilex Lane.

3 Miles, fairly level, some damp meadows.

Leave the station by a footpath going down obliquely left on the side away from the village centre. At the bottom take the footpath going directly away from the railway track to an entrance to a minor estate road. Go right along this road (Knapps Close), through the kissing gate facing you at the end, into a field.

Follow the footpath slightly left across the corner of the field of the Moose Heart residence to a similar gate on to the Banwell Road, which is joined there by Church Road. Cross carefully to reach the right hand side of Church Road.

150 yards along Church Road on the right is Nut Tree Farm with a 400 year-old history. Immediately beyond it is a lane marked 'Public Footpath', which you follow over a stile past

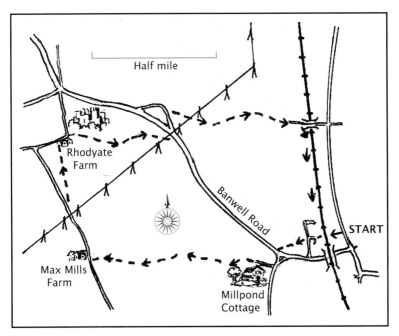

Mill Pond Cottage, the site of one of the former water mills in the Lox Yeo Valley.

At the end of the lane go left into the field and follow the path in more or less the direction you have been taking. The waymarked path takes you through several meadows with wetland flowers, to Max Mills Lane, a minor road. Almost facing you is Max Mills Farm, the site of the other former water mill.

Turn right along Max Mills Lane. Just over half a mile along the road, after passing under a line of power cables, are two signed footpaths to the right, 100 yards apart. At the second, cross a stile, bearing up left and making for a small gate to the left of Copperfield and Pickwick Cottages. Go past the houses and turn right along the road past the farm.

Where the road turns sharply left at Rhodyate Farm, leave it and continue along the lane. Up on the hill on your left is Banwell Castle which was built in 1847 as a private residence on the site of a much older farmstead. It now serves cream teas and can be reached from the Banwell Road which you cross later.

A few yards along the lane drop down into the field on the right, bear left to the gate and yellow arrow and carry on across several fields, keeping the hedge on your left until you reach the Banwell Road. Cross this road with care and go left up a loop of the old road for a few yards to a few steps up to a stile on the right. If this end of the loop road is very muddy, you can use another entrance to it further up the Banwell Road.

Over the stile, a path takes you across a field and past a pylon to a gate, and then continues gently up several fields with a hedge close on your left. Crossing a stile you enter a lane with a hedge on both sides, and after about 100 yards come to a cemetery on your right. Go through the narrow entrance on the right between the cemetery and the bridge over the railway cutting. This takes you back to the Railway Walk and the station site.

WINSCOMBE: CIRCULAR WALK 2

Tunnel - Kings Wood - Cross Plain
Hill Farm - Church Knoll

3.5 Miles, one moderate climb.

From the station site with the village centre behind you, go left, taking the bridge over the Woodborough Road and continuing for about a mile along the track under the Lynch road bridge and through the tunnel.

For a diversion avoiding the tunnel, look for a flight of steps up to the right in the cutting as you approach the tunnel. These lead you to a field owned by the Mendip Society and managed as a nature reserve, with a per-missive path up the centre. Keep to this path to a stile at the top right-hand corner on to a lane which was part of the old road to the West. Cross the road at the top of

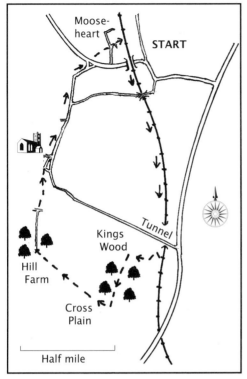

this lane to a car park at the entrance to KingsWood, where there is a National Trust information signboard. Go through the gate and take the more or less level path to the left.

At the end of the cutting beyond the tunnel, go right, making a U-turn to go up the footpath which overlooks the cutting. At the end of this path, cross the stile on your left and go through the second gate in the fence on your left into Kings Wood, owned by the National Trust.

Walk through the wood almost to the end where you will find a track on the right rising to the hillside (Cross Plain). The view on the left is of Axbridge, Cheddar and the levels. On reaching the high ground, turn right along the ridge, and you will soon see a farm (Hill Farm) among high trees.

At the farm, ignore the geese and go through a small gate to the left and down the path to Barton Drove. Slightly to the right across the drove is a gate. Go through on to the scrubby field of Church Knoll, straight over and down the hill on a winding path to Winscombe Parish Church, which dates from 1200 A.D. Go over a stile into a small field by the Old Rectory, through a kissing gate into the church yard. Turn right through the church yard leaving by the main gate.

Go left down Church Lane to the Square and continue down

Church Road for just over a mile to the Triangle at the junction with the busy Winscombe - Banwell Road.

Cross the road to a kissing gate into a field and follow the footpath to similar gate on to a small road. Cross this road on to Knapps Close where, after a few yards there is a kissing gate to a footpath up the embankment to Winscombe station site.

WINSCOMBE: CIRCULAR WALK 3

Sandford Hill - Star - Sidcot

4.5 Miles, with a moderate climb.

From the station site with the village centre behind you,go right along the old railway track. The path soon moves slightly left until it has passed a row of garden extensions which have taken over part of the railway track. Immediately beyond this set of gardens, the path goes down an incline and under a stone bridge, back on to the old railway track, now in a cutting. Follow it under a second stone bridge and for a further three quarters of a mile, where there is a flight of steps up the bank on each side.

Go up the steps on the right, over a stile and along a footpath at right angles to the railway track you have just left. This leads you to Hill Road, Sandford, where you cross to the Methodist Chapel and turn left. Just below the Church Hall, a road rises to the right. Keep bearing right, then ascend a grassy slope to the left of Batch House, into woods. Over a stile turn left and follow the woodland path until it eventually turns right and meets a crossing path at a stile.

Go through the gate to your left and take the stile facing you on the right of the path. Your route goes slightly to the right to a gap in the hedge. Continue in the same direction, then downhill to a stile in the bottom corner of the field. Go straight down this field to Pylewell Lane where you turn left and soon through a gate, the path taking you to the A38 at Star.

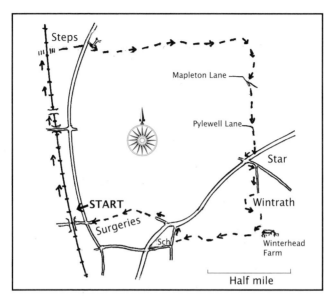

Turn right along the A38 to the crossroads and left over the road, with great care, towards Shipham, and 100 yards up on the right follow Horseleaze Lane to a stile on to rough open ground.

Follow the footpath to the right and round the edge of the field into a lane. Turn left down to crossing paths and go over these towards the farm. Look out for the gate below the farm on the right. The path from here is well signed to a track below the cattle grid. Cross and take the gate to the left. The path now takes you towards Sidcot School. At the end of the penultimate field you climb rough steps to a stile hidden in a hedge.

Turn right through the gate and then obliquely left across the field to a second gate, go a few yards down the tarmac lane, then turn right to the A38. Cross this busy road to the tarmac surfaced Hillyfields Lane. Follow this lane down to a kissing gate into a field and continue in the same direction with the hedge on your left, through another kissing gate, past the surgeries and the Woodborough. Ahead of you the Woodborough Road leads down towards the old railway bridge and your starting point.

WINSCOMBE: CIRCULAR WALK 4

The Grove - Mill Pond Cottage - Max Mills
Barton Drove - Kings Wood - Tunnel

5 Miles, fairly level, can be very wet in places.

From the station site, with the village behind you, go right along the railway track. Soon the path is diverted slightly to the left to avoid garden extensions. Just after the second of these gardens, cross the stile on the left and follow the path across the fields as it swings gradually to the left to enter a lane, and follow this to the Banwell Road.

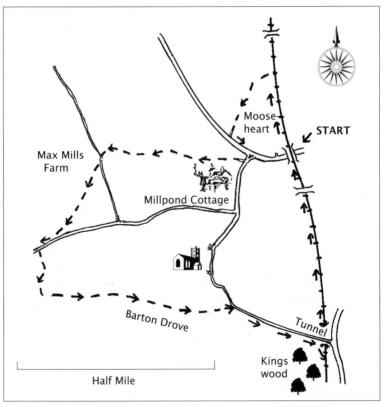

Turn left along the Banwell Road and cross it as it reaches the Triangle, a little group of trees at the junction with Church Road. 150 yards along Church Road on the right just past Nut Tree Farm is a lane marked 'Public Footpath'. Follow this lane over a stile past Mill Pond Cottage, the site of one of the former water mills in the Lox Yeo Valley.

At the end of the lane go left into the field and follow the path in more or less the direction you have been taking. The waymarked path takes you through several meadows with wetland flowers, to Max Mills Lane, a minor road.

Almost facing you is Max Mills Farm, the site of the other former water mill. Cross the road, go left and, after 30 yards, turn right over a stile marked 'public footpath'. Follow the path, which goes obliquely left across the field. Stop at the gate and look back to see the south elevation of Max Mills Farmhouse, a Grade 2 listed building. Continue along the path to Barton Road.

Turn right along Barton Road, then after 200 yards turn left up a tarmac surfaced lane marked 'Footpath'. The lane with a hedge on each side climbs steeply for 300 yards. At the point where the lane bears right into a garden, follow the narrow footpath for about 50 yards to reach Barton Drove. Go left along Barton Drove until, after nearly a mile, it joins a road, Winscombe Hill. Continue in the same direction for about half a mile to a car park on the right.

For a diversion avoiding the tunnel, go down the lane on the left just before the car park and after about 100 yards cross the stile on the right into the field owned by the Mendip Society and managed as a nature reserve. This has a permissive path down the centre to a stile leading to a short flight of steps down into the railway cutting, where you turn left on to the track.

At the car park go through the gates by the National Trust information signboard, and then left with the fence on your left to a stile signposted Railway Walk. Follow the sloping path down and turn left at the railway track, now a cycleway. This takes you through the tunnel, past the Recreation Ground, under the Lynch Road Bridge and over the Woodborough Road, back to the station site.

WINSCOMBE: CIRCULAR WALK 5

Sandford Hill - Star - Shipham - Shute Shelve - Tunnel

6.5 Miles, several climbs and some stretches which are very muddy in wet weather, with some magnificent views and very varied terrain.

From the station site with the village centre behind you go right, following the path until it descends at the end of the garden extensions. Do not follow it down, but continue on the footpath above the cutting, coming out on to Ilex Lane.

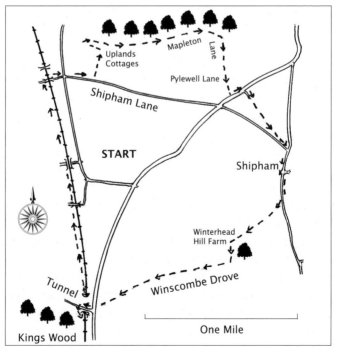

Turn right over the bridge to Sandford Road, cross the road to Shipham Lane and follow it to a drive on the left signposted 'Uplands Cottages'. Go up the drive until it turns right towards the houses, when you carry straight on up a grassy slope to a small wooden gate at the wood edge.

Enter the wood, turn left and follow the track with a fence on the left for a quarter of a mile to a house, then turn sharp right on to a major track climbing the flank of the hill and follow this track with a fence on the left for three quarters of a mile.

Avoid the lower track and follow the main track which climbs gently through the wood, while open spaces of heathland can be seen through a substantial chain-link fence on the left. Traces of a much older trackway with double banks can be seen on the right. Where the track emerges on to open fields at a gateway, continue in the same direction along the track.

Where the track begins to descend, bear right and go through the gate on the right (bridleway waymark) which indicates the beginning of Lyncombe Lane. 160 yards down the lane, where a footpath and several gates open on to it, turn sharply right on to Mapleton Lane, another of the ancient trackways on Sandford Hill. At the foot of the slope are two derelict kilns. At a building on the right, the lane merges with Pylewell Lane, to continue to the A38.

Turn left along the A38 for 100 yards and cross with great care to Cheddarcombe Lane which goes up between houses of the hamlet of Star. The lane soon becomes a footpath continuing up the combe towards Shipham, emerging next to the old turnpike tollhouse.

In Shipham refreshment is available at the Miners Arms, and at the Penscot Hotel in the village square.

At the tollhouse, cross to the pavement on the right of the road and go to the centre of the old lead-mining village of Shipham, passing the school and the Miners Arms. Your route continues in the same direction up Cuck Hill, where it is safer to use the raised footpath on the left of the road. Where this ends, cross the road and go down a few yards to some steps up to a stile with a post marked 'West Mendip Way', a route you will be on for some distance.

Over the stile, go down to the bridge over the stream and up the other side to a stile taking you into a field. On your left in this field are remains of an old trackway, while over to the right on a fine day are views across to the hills of Wales

Keeping to the hedge on your right, cross the field to a stone stile and cross the next field to a gate into the lane above Winterhead Hill Farm. Go left up this lane to Winscombe Drove, then right along the drove for about a mile, when you reach the A38, still following 'West Mendip Way' signs. Cross the A38 at the traffic island by the garage, go left to a road, Winscombe Hill, and along it to a car park on the left.

For a diversion avoiding the tunnel, go down the lane on the right opposite the car park, as described in Winscombe Walk 4.

In the car park go through the gate by the National Trust signboard and down to, and over a stile in the fence on the left on to Railway Walk land. Follow the sloping path down to the old railway track, now a cycleway.

Turn very sharp left along the track and follow it through the tunnel, past Winscombe Recreation Ground, under The Lynch road bridge, over the Woodborough Road, back to the station site.

Winscombe Church.

WALKS FROM THE AXBRIDGE BY-PASS

The starting point is the lay-by on the Axbridge by-pass between Cheddar and the A38 (GR423547). This has a car park, an information board and a picnic area. The car park can be full on Summer weekends. To reach it without a car:

On Foot: From Axbridge Square go the length of High Street and its continuation, West Street to the bus stop at Compton Cottage, just beyond Compton House on the left. Cross to the slip road signposted 'Weston-super-Mare/Bristol' and go up for 300 yards where a short path on the right just before the main road takes you on to the lay-by

By Bus: The 126 (Weston-super-Mare - Wells), getting out at Compton Cottage, between Axbridge and Cross, where the by-pass slip roads come down to the bus route. Go up the slip road signposted 'Weston-super-Mare/ Bristol' as above.

Axbridge Square with King John's Hunting Lodge.

AXBRIDGE BY-PASS: CIRCULAR WALK 1

Prowse Lane - Cross Moor Drove West -
Bourton Farm - Hill Farm - Kings Wood - Tunnel

4 miles, one substantial climb.

With the by-pass on your right, go to the end of the lay-by and down the slip road to Cross Lane at the bottom. Cross this road to the lane to Townsend Farm, ignoring the stile in the fence on your right. Your route passes to the left of the farm and turns slightly right into Prowse Lane where it continues on the right hand side of a rhyne for half a mile, where you meet the Cheddar Yeo at right angles.

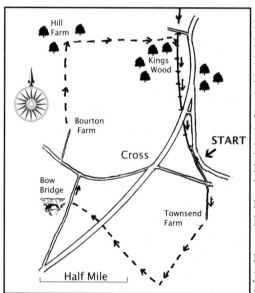

Cross and turn right along the Yeo, recrossing where necessary until you reach the A38. Cross the A38 with care and continue along the path (Cross Moor Drove, West) on the right hand side of the Yeo until you reach a minor road at Bow Bridge.

Go right along the road to the T junction, then left for 300 yards to Bourton Lane which goes up on the right. Go up Bourton Lane to Bourton Farm, turn left at the farm, past Bourton Cottage and through the gate. Turn right up the path to Wavering Down, climbing steadily, past a wooden post marked 'Winscombe/

98

Cross', making for Hill Farm in a group of high trees.

At Hill Farm, do not go through the gate, but turn right along the path going downhill for a mile with a stone wall on your left. This wall marks an old adminisrative boundary dating from Saxon times, continuing from Crook Peak behind you and over Shute Shelve and Callow Hill ahead. It is currently a county boundary, dividing Winscombe in North Somerset from Compton Bishop in Somerset County.

On reaching the National Trust signboard, gates and car park, do not go through the gates but turn right down to a stile in the fence on your left. Go over the stile into Railway Walk land and down the path to the railway track, now a cycleway. Continue in the same direction along the cycleway, crossing the A38 carefully at the chicane, and continuing up the other side, back to your starting point on the Axbridge by-pass.

AXBRIDGE BY-PASS: CIRCULAR WALK 2

Callow Hill - Winscombe Drove - Shipham - Winterhead - Winscombe - Tunnel

7 Miles, one substantial climb, magnificent views.
An option 4.5 miles long omits Shipham, Winterhead and Winscombe village.

From the signboard on the lay-by, cross the Axbridge slip-road and continue along the verge of the main road (by-pass) for a short distance until you see a gate on the right hand side of the road.

Cross the road carefully, go over the stile following the footpath with the fence on the right and pass a quarry on the left to reach a stile on the right. Cross over the stile and go down through allotments/strawberry fields to a fence. You are now above Axbridge.

Follow the footpath left, walking alongside the fence,

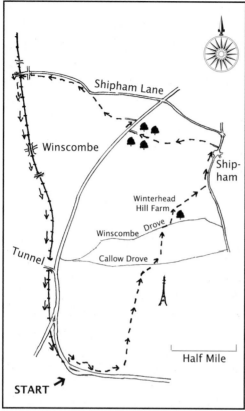

through a gate to a small car park. Continue past the homes of Hillside, down a lane nearly to the by-pass.

Turn left up the hill on to quite a steep track, which after a while levels out. Ignore the steps down to Axbridge Station and the Vinery, which are opposite the house called 'Overlake'. Follow the track up to the left. You now have a good view of the town and vine-yard. Go through a stile and continue on the track which rises for some distance, until you meet a triple junction of footpaths.

Go straight on into the wood along the footpath with an ancient wall on the right. Keep climbing (the path is slippery if wet), and near the top of the hill go over the wall at a stile and turn left up the hill, with the wall now on the left. The path climbs steeply past 'gruffy ground' of old mines in a field, mostly on the right.

From the top of the hill and for most of the way to Shipham on a clear day you have magnificent views across the Bristol Channel seeing, according to the particular vantage point, the islands of Steepholm and Flatholm, the Welsh hills and the Second Severn Bridge. At the hilltop, cross over the path leading to the mast and over a double stile, the path continuing by a wall on your left to a stile. It then veers right, away from the wall towards Callow Drove, to a gap in the wall of the drove about one third of the way along the boundary of the field you are crossing. Cross Callow Drove and leave it by the stile, when the path veers right towards woodland. Here the path goes steeply down a narrow ravine wooded on both sides. It then continues with a hedge on the left, over a field, to a stile on to Winscombe Drove.

Your route now takes you through the old lead-mining village of Shipham. An alternative, two and a half miles shorter, will take you directly to Winscombe.

To take the shorter route, go straight across and leave the drove by the stile opposite, following the path down the valley opening up in front of you. After another stile pass woodland on the left and take the signed path up the hill where the woods end. At the top turn right 45 degrees and cross the field to a gate on to Oakridge Lane. Go down the lane to a signed footpath on the left between a house called Shortwood and one called Shute Field. This takes you alongside gardens down to the A38. Cross this main road and go along Fullers Lane opposite until it bends left. Go over the stile on the right, along the path between gardens and the cricket ground, and down the flight of old railway steps on to the Railway Walk and Cycleway. Turn left along it, through the tunnel and back to your starting point.

If you wish to go through Shipham, turn right along Winscombe Drove for 150 yards before taking the track on the left leading to Winterhead Hill Farm. About 250 yards down, just past the trees on the right and before the farm buildings on the left, go through a gate on the right into a field. Cross the field, walking uphill roughly parallel to the wood boundary, and cross a stone slab stile set in the hedge. In the next field, follow the line of the hedge on your left and cross a stile in front of you at the corner of the field, just past the point where the path is crossed by an old trackway. The path then goes steeply down to a stream, over a bridge and up the other side to a stile on to Cuck Lane, Shipham, a quite busy road

It is safer here to go up the hill for a few yards to the right before crossing to a raised footpath on the other side and go down this path to Shipham, where refreshments are available at the Penscot Hotel in the Square and at the Miners Arms ust beyond. Continue through the square and past the Miners Arms, turning left down Comrade Avenue. At the bottom, go through a chicane on to a path in the same direction, down to the hamlet of Winterhead. Here continue in more or less the same direction through an avenue of trees, mainly beech and scots pine. Just above you on the right is the house 'Wintrath', once the home of E F Knight, author of many books on Mendip. The avenue of trees ends at the A38, which must be crossed with great care.

Go right along the pavement of the A38 and, after about 200 yards, opposite the lodge and entrance of Queensmead Court, take the lane on the left with hedges on both sides and lilies of the valley and wild garlic below. This lane leads to fields where you continue just left of the hedge until Shipham Lane, a minor road.

Go left along Shipham Lane, then cross the busier Sandford Road to Ilex Lane, where you cross the bridge over the railway cutting. Immediately past the bridge go through the small chicane on you left to the footpath above the cutting. This leads to the Railway Walk and Cycleway where you continue through Winscombe Station and the tunnel and over the A38 back to your starting point.

WALKS FROM CHEDDAR

CHEDDAR: CIRCULAR WALK 1

Cycleway - Cheddar Wood - Hillside - Axbridge Square - Boatyard.

4.5 miles, one moderate climb, with fairly dry ground as a rule.

The southern entrance to the cycleway is on Station Road (GR455532). The Bus route is the 126, stopping at Church Street, near the Market Cross in the centre of the old village (GR459532).
Refreshments: at the Bath Arms in Bath Street and many places throughout Cheddar.

For this walk, from the Market Cross go along Bath Street, past the Bath Arms, continuing along Station Road, passing left of the War Memorial. About 250 yards past the War Memorial take a turning right signed 'Valley Line Industrial Park'. At the end of this short road is the entry to the Axbridge-Cheddar Cycleway. Go through the chicane on to the Cycleway and go its entire length.

At the end, cross the main road with care and turn right along the pavement. After 200 yards take the lane on the left and walk on up the slope past the entrance to 'The Parsonage'. Climb the stile at the end of the lane into Cheddar Wood Nature Reserve.

In the reserve, carry on along the footpath, through the hunting gate at the end and take the waymarked footpath to the left.

After 200 yards take the rather indistinct footpath which strikes across the hill to the right. During the Summer you

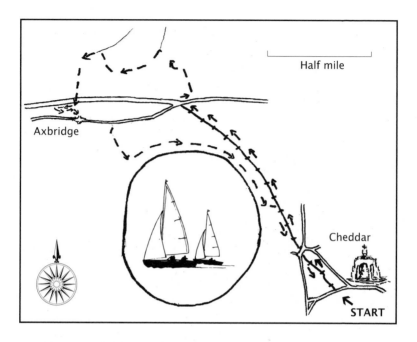

Half mile

Axbridge

Cheddar

START

may have to look carefully for this path. A steady climb for nearly half a mile brings you to a junction with a track coming down the hill. Join this track on its downward path to the left, climb the stile and take the waymarked footpath along the hillside until, after crossing one more stile, you come to the the main road (the Axbridge by-pass).

Cross the road with care and go through the narrow opening opposite by the road signs, turn immediately left and follow the lane down past St John's Church into Axbridge Town Square. Among the old buildings in this former administrative centre is the 14th century house known as 'King John's Hunting Lodge', currently a museum of local history.

Leave the square by St Mary's Street and pass a garage on your left and Parkfield Road on your right. Soon after this is a 'Public Footpath' sign on the right immediately after a bungalow named 'Mendip View'.

Follow the signed footpath to the end where there are two gates side by side. Go through the left hand one, cross the field, go over the stile and immediately turn left. Cross one more stile, then follow the track through the trees to the entrance road to Cheddar Reservoir.

Pass through the kissing gate and walk up the slope to the edge of the reservoir, turn left along the perimeter road and follow it past the sailing club until the start of the sports field down the bank on your left. Descend the bank, cross the stile and follow the track which leads back to the Cycleway. At the Cycleway, turn right and retrace your steps to Station Road, Cheddar.

CHEDDAR: CIRCULARWALK 2

Middle Moor Lane - Stubbington Drove - Cradle Bridge - Ellenge Stream - Cycleway.

6 miles, level ground, can be wet and muddy in places. In a wet summer, lush growth of tall grass and crops can make the path very narrow.

This walk starts at the Recreation Ground car park at the far end of Sharpham Road (GR 449535).

To get there from the Market Cross, go along Bath Road and Station Road as far as the War Memorial, then slightly right along Wideatts Road then left, crossing Fiveways Bridge over the old Railway Line. Sharpham Road is immediately on the right.

On leaving the car park turn right down Middle Moor Drove, a bridleway which skirts the outer southern perimeter of Cheddar Reservoir. Continue into Stubbington Drove, leaving the Angling Club car park on your right. At the end of Stubbington Drove, cross a hump-backed bridge over the Cheddar Yeo, go left for about 35 yards, then right with the rhyne on your left. Continue in the same direction past a farm gate and past the pumping station which regulates the water

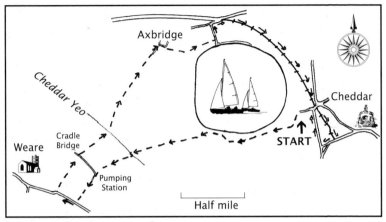

levels in the rhynes in the area.

From the pumping station take the lane slightly to the left to Frogshole Farm and on to Brinscombe Lane, a minor road. Turn right along Brinscombe Lane for about 250 yards to Stream Farm.

A diversion of about one third of a mile further along the road will take you to the 15th Century church of St Gregory in the village of Weare.

Go through the gate on the left of Stream Farm and across the field with the hedge on your right to Cradle Bridge, and after a quarter of a mile reach the Cheddar Yeo.

Cross the Cheddar Yeo and continue in the same direction with the Ellenge Stream on your right for about three quarters of a mile. Soon after passing the sewage works on the right, you reach a road. Here you turn right with Axbridge First school on your left. Turn right at the end of the road and again left immediately before Moorland Farm. Carry on along the lane until it takes a right angled bend to the right. At this point you will see a gate and stile in front of you. Climb the stile and follow the footpath which takes you round the north side of the reservoir, where a quarter of a mile after passing the pumping station on your right, you turn left, up the access

106

road to the the reservoir which takes you to Cheddar Road. Turn right along this road until, just after it joins a main road, you go through the entrance on the right to the Axbridge-Cheddar Cycleway. Along the cycleway you see the reservoir on your right, then go through the cutting. Immediately before Fiveways Bridge, the old railway bridge taking the Wedmore Road over the line, are the remains on the right, of a stone loading platform. The steps up there lead on to Sharpham Road, but this is not an official access point, as it crosses private land. The correct route is under Fiveways Bridge, along the fenced Track through the industrial estate on to Station Road. Here you go right until the T junction, right again along Lower New Road to Sharpham Road on the left, just before Fiveways Bridge.

Cheddar Market Cross.

THE ROAD
(With acknowledgements to Sir Harry Lauder)

We're leaving behind us the signals and rails,
And turning our backs on the trains.
On the left and right hand we see miles of flat land
Divided by ditches and drains.
Alders and willows rise out of the hedge
Of blackthorn and hawthorn and briar,
With cinquefoil and bugloss and hawkweed and teazel
Up on the track where it's drier.

The ditches, called rhynes, need special machines
To keep them sufficiently deep,
For only the drainage provides the dry land
As pasture for cattle and sheep.
Clusters of kingcups and iris and reeds
Have tadpoles and beetles between.
Mussels and snails and larvae with tails
All make up the life of the rhyne.

Quite soon we're in woodland, with oak and with ash,
High up on the bank as we ramble.
It's here that we gather with billhooks to slash,
And clear the way through past the bramble.
The dogwood, the hazel, the hawthorn, the rose
Need trimming, that's just making thinner.
With elder and sloe, they all need to grow -
For everything's somebody's dinner.

Do we halt at the station? No, not any more!
Once it gave us the centre for shopping.
Today we just dream of the great age of steam,
Of puffing and hooting and stopping.
A platform and coal dust are all that remains,
And a view that is almost a town,
Where the traffic is slowed on a busy main road,
By the bridge that they meant to knock down.

We enter the hill where they started to dig -
The men who created the track -
Who'd made their way in, leaving village and kin,
Where hope for the future looked black.
The prize they could get with their muscle and sweat.
Was their keep, and a little to spend,
As they cut through the hill with their powder and drill,
To reach to the light at the end.

South of the tunnel are bare rocky walls
With mosses and ferns to the floor,
Then down the banks go to the pastures below,
Which reach to the hills and the moor.
On the track we have marjoram, trefoil and vetch,
With gatekeepers, skippers and browns,
Till the path falls again to the watery plain,
As we come to the old Saxon towns.

Over our heads fly the geese and the teal,
Past the boats with their rods and their sails.
The views of the levels reach out to the hills,
And across to the mountains of Wales.
We've left far behind us the wayfaring tree,
The tunnel, the pond and the toad.
Ahead are the bells of the City of Wells,
Aloft at the end of the road.

CHRONICLE

Railway

1867 February 26	'First sod' (by Bristol & Exeter)
1869 August3	Reached Cheddar
1875 November	Change to Broad Gauge
1876 June 1	Great Western Railway takeover
1901 November 23	Wrington Vale Line opened
1947	British Rail Vesting
1952	Wrington Vale Line closed
1963 August 7	Last regular passenger train

Walkway and Cycleway

1975-6	First approach to British Rail
1977 July	Group approach to British Rail
1977 November	Petition to Woodspring D.C.
1978 February 20	Inaugural Meeting of Society
1978 April 3	Winscombe Parish A.G.M. approval
1978 September 13	Approach from Cyclebag
1979 February 8	First A.G.M. of Society
1979 February 19	British Rail to sell Line
1980	Joint Proposal with Cyclebag
1981 November 17	Woodspring decision to buy
1983 April	Woodspring purchase completed
1985	Shute Shelve purchase (British Rail)
1987 June	Axbridge-Cheddar Cycleway Planning
1989 January	Axbridge-Cheddar Cycleway Start
1990 October 21	Axbridge-Cheddar Cycleway Opened
1994 April	Feasibility study (cycling) proposal
1994	Wemberham Triangle SSSI
1996 February	Feasibility study carried out
1996 June3	Shute Shelve (Arbour) purchase
1996 Spring	Yatton - A38 Cycling agreed by CVRWS
1996 Summer	Yatton - A38 Cycling agreed by Woodspring
1996 September	Local Nature Reserve approval
1997 March	Cycling conversion started
1997 June 10	Cycleway opened to Winscombe
1998 Jan - Feb	Ramp at Ilex Lane constructed
1998 February 20	Yatton Station Purchase
1998 Summer	Sandford Permissive Path
1999 February 27	Millennium Green 'First Sod'
1999 Feb-March	Yatton Station connecting path

SOURCES AND FURTHER READING

History of the Railway
Clinker, C.R. (1950) 'The Cheddar Valley Railway'. *The Railway Magazine* 96, No 588, p. 224.
Clinker, C.R. (1969) *The Cheddar Valley Railway*. Sidcot Old Scholars Report, p.46-51.
Congresbury History Group (1986) *The Railway at Congresbury*
Farr, M., Maggs. C.G., Lovell, R. & Whetmath, C. (1978) *The Wrington Vale Light Railway*. Avon-Anglia.
Madge, R. (1984) *Somerset Railways*. Dovecote.
Mitchell, V. & Smith, K. (1997) *Branch Line to Cheddar Including the Wrington Vale Light Railway*. Middleton Press.
Newman, E.W. (1919) *Francis Fox & John Hingston Fox*. Sidcot School Register of Old Scholars 1808-1912. p. 70 & 72. Percival Jones Ltd., Birmingham.
Robertson, K. (1990) *Somerset and Avon Railways in Old Photographs*. Alan Sutton.
Vintner, J. (1990) *Railway Walks GWR & SR*. Alan Sutton.

History of the Railway Walk
Avon Wildlife Trust (1997) *Cheddar Valley Railway Walk Management Plan*. North Somerset Council.
Brenchley,L., Brenchley, N., Day, R., Lister, M., MacNicol, S., Pegler, A., Richmond, D., Richmond, U. & Russell, R. (1978) *Cheddar Valley Railway Walk - a Proposal*. Winscombe Parish Council Railway Walk Committee.
Cyclebag & Cheddar Valley Railway Walk Society (1979) *Yatton to Axbridge and Cheddar - a Project to Walk and Cycle along the Disused Cheddar Valley Railway*.
Landmark Environmental Consultants (1996) *Cheddar Valley Railway Feasibility Study*. Woodspring District Council.
Woodspring District Council (1995) *North Somerset Countryside Strategy*

Plants & Animals
Appleton, J.H. & Appleton, R.J. (1970) *Disused Railways in the Countryside of England and Wales*. H.M.S.O..London.
Avon Wildlife Trust (1997) *Cheddar Valley Railway Survey*, 1997. North Somerset Council.
Dower, M. (1963) *Greenways: a Future for Britain's Cast-off Railways*. Architectural Revue, 134, p. 387-394.
English Nature (1991) *Avon Levels and Moors: Report of a Ditch Survey*.
Green, B.(1981) Countryside *Conservation, the Protection and Management of Amenity Ecosystems*. The Resource Management Series 3, Second Edition. Unwin Hyman, London.
Grimshaw, J. & Associates (1982) *Disused Railways in England and Wales. Potential Cycle Routes*. H.M.S.O., London.
Ingle, R. (1995) *Past, Present and Future Management of the Disused Cheddar Valley Railway Line; a Possible Nature Reserve*. University of Plymouth.
Mitchell, D.N. & Cooke, J.A. (1991) *The Current Status of Plant Ecology of Disused Railway Lines in North Tyneside*. Transactions of the Natural History Society, Northumbria, 55,4.273-282.

Sargent, C. (1984) *Britain's Railway Vegetation*. Institute of Terrestrial Ecology, Monkswood.

Somerville, C. (1979) *Walking Old Railways*. David & Charles.

Weston-super-Mare RSPB Local Members Group (1994,95,96,97,98) North *Somerset Levels Birds Survey*.

Weston-super-Mare RSPB Local Members Group (1995,96,97,98) *North Somerset Levels Breeding Birds Survey*.

Winscombe Parish Council (1998) *Millennium Green: a Proposal*.

Geology

Alabaster, C. (1982) *The Minerals of Mendip*. Somerset Mines Research Group,1, (4).

Farrant, A.R. & Smart, P.L. (1997) *The Geomorphic Evolution of the Mendip Hills*. Bristol Naturalists' Society, 55, p. 135-158.

Simms, M.J. (1997) *The Geological History of the Mendip Hills and their Margins*. Bristol Naturalists' Society, 55, p. 113-134.

Stanton, W.I. (1991) *The Habitat and Origin of Lead Ore in Grebe Swallet Mine,Charterhouse-on-Mendip, Somerset*. Proceedings of the University of Bristol Speleological Society, 19 (1), p 43-65.

Whittaker, A. & Green, G.W. (1983) *Geology of the Country around Weston-super-Mare*. Memoir of Geological Survey of Great Britain, HMSO.